© *[2024]* **Evan Rhodes**

All rights reserved. No part of this book may be reproduced, in any form or by any means, including electronic, mechanical, photocopying, recording, or otherwise, without the prior written permission of the publisher, except for brief excerpts used in reviews.

Disclaimer: The information contained in this book is for educational purposes only. While every effort has been made to ensure the accuracy of the content, the author and publisher disclaim any responsibility for errors or omissions. Readers are encouraged to seek professional advice where needed.

Android Game Development with Kotlin

A Beginner-to-Advanced Guide to Mastering Game Design

By
Evan Rhodes

Contents

Introduction 2

Part 1: Getting Started with Kotlin and Android Development 11

Chapter 1: Setting Up Your Development Environment 12

1.1 Installing Android Studio 12

1.2 Configuring Kotlin for Android Projects 22

1.3 Overview of Development Tools and Resources 33

Project: Create Your First "Hello, Game!" App 46

Chapter 2: Kotlin Fundamentals for Game Developers 61

2.1 Variables, Data Types, and Control Flow 61

2.2 Functions, Classes, and Object-Oriented Programming 73

2.3 Handling User Input and Events 90

Project: Build a Basic Calculator App.109

Chapter 3: Understanding the Android Framework 130

   3.1 Activities, Fragments, and the Android Lifecycle................................. 130

   3.2 Creating and Managing Layouts for Games 151

   3.3 Basics of XML and Views in Android 172

   Project: Design a Simple App Layout with Interactive Buttons 186

Part 2: Game Design Fundamentals 203

   Chapter 4: Introduction to Game Design 204

      4.1 Key Elements of Game Mechanics 205

      4.2 Understanding Sprites, Animation, and Physics 223

      4.3 Planning Your First Game 238

Project: Storyboard a Simple Game Idea (Paper-Based Exercise) 249

Chapter 5: Creating Your First 2D Game 266

    5.1 Setting Up a Game Loop 266

    5.2 Drawing Sprites and Handling Collisions 283

    5.3 Adding User Interactivity 301

    Project: Build a Simple "Catch the Ball" Game 321

Chapter 6: Working with Graphics and Animations 345

    6.1 Customizing Canvas and Drawing API 345

    6.2 Using Bitmap and Vector Assets in Your Games 363

    6.3 Animating Objects for Dynamic Gameplay 375

    Project: Add Animation to Your "Catch the Ball" Game 390

Part 3: Advanced Game Development Techniques 409

Chapter 7: Building More Complex Games 410

7.1 Managing Multiple Levels and Game States 410

7.2 Advanced Input Handling (Gestures, Multi-Touch, etc.) 427

7.3 Adding Power-Ups, Enemies, and Scoring 447

Project: Develop a Multi-Level Platformer Game 465

Chapter 8: Integrating Sound and Music 488

8.1 Adding Background Music and Sound Effects 488

8.2 Managing Audio Resources Efficiently 503

Project: Enhance Your Platformer Game with Sound Effects 506

Chapter 9: Optimizing Game Performance 520

9.1 Reducing Lag and Improving FPS 520

9.2 Memory Management Tips...........527

9.3 Testing and Debugging Games 532

Project: Debug and Optimize Your Platformer Game for Smoother Gameplay................534

Part 4: Publishing and Monetizing Your Game 549

Chapter 10: Preparing Your Game for Release...................550

10.1 Testing Your Game on Multiple Devices.................550

10.2 Finalizing Graphics and Sound Quality.................554

Project: Final Testing and Packaging Your Platformer Game 557

Chapter 11: Publishing to Google Play Store 562

11.1 Creating a Developer Account....562

11.2 App Bundles and APK Files........564

11.3 Writing an Effective App Description...566

Project: Submit Your Platformer Game to the Play Store 567

Chapter 12: Monetizing Your Game.......571

12.1 Implementing Ads 571

12.2 Setting Up In-App Purchases......578

12.3 Exploring Alternative Revenue Streams...582

Part 5: Expanding Your Skills...............584

Chapter 13: Exploring 3D Game Development Basics 585

Introduction to 3D Graphics in Android 585

Tools and Frameworks for 3D Games 604

Appendices 621

Appendix A: Troubleshooting Common Errors 621

Appendix B: Sample Game Code and Links 624

Appendix C: Glossary of Key Terms ..626

Introduction

Welcome to *Android Game Development with Kotlin*! Whether you're dreaming of creating your own mobile game or you're already an aspiring developer looking to sharpen your skills, this book is designed to guide you from beginner to advanced levels in Android game design.

In this chapter, we'll explore why Android game development is such an exciting field, why **Kotlin** is the perfect language for the job, and what you can expect to learn throughout this book.

Why Build Android Games?

Android is one of the most popular mobile platforms worldwide, powering billions of devices. Mobile gaming is a huge industry, generating billions of dollars in revenue annually. If you've ever thought about diving into game development, the Android ecosystem offers several compelling advantages:

- **Massive Reach**: With Android's global market share, your games can reach a vast audience.
- **Creative Freedom**: Android's open-source nature allows developers to explore and innovate freely.
- **Diverse Monetization Options**: From ads and in-app purchases to premium apps, Android provides plenty of ways to make your games profitable.

Take, for instance, simple yet wildly successful games like *Flappy Bird* or *Crossy Road*. These games were built with straightforward mechanics but captivated millions of players. You don't need a massive budget or a large team to succeed; what you need is creativity, dedication, and the right tools—this book will provide you with those tools.

Kotlin: The Ideal Language for Game Development

Kotlin is Google's preferred language for Android development, and for good reason:

1. **Ease of Use: Kotlin**'s concise and readable syntax makes it beginner-friendly, reducing the boilerplate code you often encounter with Java.
2. **Performance: Kotlin** compiles to Java bytecode, ensuring your games run efficiently on Android devices.
3. **Interoperability: Kotlin** works seamlessly with Java, so you can leverage existing Android libraries and frameworks.
4. **Modern Features**: With features like null safety and coroutines, **Kotlin** helps

you write robust and efficient code, critical for smooth and bug-free games.

Here's a quick example to showcase **Kotlin**'s simplicity:

Kotlin

```
// Traditional Java example
public void displayMessage(String message) {

System.out.println(message);
}

// Kotlin equivalent
fun displayMessage(message: String) {
    println(message)
}
```

Notice how much cleaner and shorter the **Kotlin** code is. That's the beauty of **Kotlin**— it lets you focus on building features rather than wrestling with syntax.

What You'll Learn from This Book

This book is your companion for mastering Android game development using **Kotlin**. Here's a glimpse of the journey ahead:

- **Getting Started**: Learn to set up your development environment, master **Kotlin** basics, and dive into the Android framework.
- **Design Fundamentals**: Understand game mechanics, animation, and physics to create engaging experiences.
- **Hands-On Projects**: Build games like *Catch the Ball* and a multi-level platformer as you learn.

- **Advanced Techniques**: Optimize game performance, integrate sound, and manage complex game states.
- **Publishing and Monetizing**: Prepare your game for release on the Google Play Store and explore monetization strategies.

Practical Example: A Simple Kotlin App

To give you a taste of what's to come, let's create a simple Android app that displays "Welcome to Game Development!" on the screen.

1. **Step 1: Setting Up Your Environment**
   Ensure you have Android Studio installed. Create a new project and select "Empty Activity" as your template.

Step 2: Writing Kotlin Code
In your `MainActivity.kt` file, replace the default code with the following:
Kotlin

```
package com.example.gamedevelopment

import android.os.Bundle
import android.widget.TextView
import androidx.appcompat.app.AppCompatActivity

class MainActivity : AppCompatActivity() {
    override fun onCreate(savedInstanceState: Bundle?) {
```

```kotlin
        super.onCreate(savedInstanceState)
        // Set up a TextView programmatically
        val textView = TextView(this)
        textView.text = "Welcome to Game Development!"
        textView.textSize = 24f

textView.textAlignment = TextView.TEXT_ALIGNMENT_CENTER

        // Set the content view to this TextView
setContentView(textView)
    }
```

}

2. **Step 3: Running the App**
   Run the app on an emulator or a physical Android device. You'll see the message displayed prominently on the screen.

Part 1: Getting Started with Kotlin and Android Development

Chapter 1: Setting Up Your Development Environment

Welcome to the first step in your Android game development journey! Before we dive into creating fun and engaging games, we need to ensure your development environment is set up correctly. This chapter will guide you through installing Android Studio, configuring **Kotlin** for your projects, and familiarizing yourself with essential tools and resources. By the end of this chapter, you'll create your first "Hello, Game!" app.

1.1 Installing Android Studio

Before diving into Android game development, it's essential to set up the right tools. The backbone of Android development is **Android Studio**, Google's official Integrated Development Environment (IDE).

It offers all the features you need to build, test, and debug your Android games efficiently. In this section, I'll walk you through the process of downloading, installing, and configuring Android Studio step by step.

Why Android Studio?

Android Studio provides:

- A **powerful code editor** with **Kotlin** support, making it perfect for game development.
- Integrated tools like the **Android Emulator**, allowing you to test games without a physical device.
- Built-in templates and wizards to speed up development.

Step 1: Downloading Android Studio

1. **Visit the Official Android Studio Website**
   Go to the official Android Studio download page.
2. **Choose Your Platform**
   - For **Windows**: Download the `.exe` installer.
   - For **macOS**: Download the `.dmg` installer.
   - For **Linux**: Download the `.zip` file.

   Pro Tip: Always download the latest stable version to ensure compatibility with current tools and SDKs.

Step 2: Installing Android Studio

For Windows

1. Run the downloaded `.exe` file.
2. Follow the installation wizard:
   - Accept the license agreement.
   - Select the installation location.
   - Choose components to install (leave defaults checked for beginners).
3. Click **Install** and wait for the process to complete.

For macOS

1. Open the downloaded `.dmg` file.
2. Drag the Android Studio icon into the Applications folder.
3. Open Android Studio from the Applications folder.

For Linux

Extract the `.zip` file to a location of your choice:

bash

```
unzip android-studio-*.zip
```

1.

Navigate to the `bin` directory and launch the installer:

bash

```
./studio.sh
```

Step 3: Initial Setup

Once installed, launch Android Studio. The first-time setup wizard will guide you through the process:

1. **Welcome Screen**
   Click **Next** to proceed with the setup.
2. **Install SDK Components**
   - Android Studio will prompt you to install the Android SDK, Emulator, and necessary libraries.
   - Select the default options for a seamless setup.
3. **Choose UI Theme**
   Select a theme for the editor—**Light** or **Dark** (personal preference).
4. **Download Components**
   The wizard will download required files based on your selections. This may take a few minutes, depending on your internet speed.

Step 4: Verify the Installation

To ensure everything is working:

1. Open Android Studio.

2. Click on **New Project** and select the "Empty Activity" template.
3. Set the language to **Kotlin** and click **Finish**.
4. Once the project loads, click the green "Run" button (play icon) in the toolbar.
    - If you've set up everything correctly, a blank app will run on the emulator or a connected device.

Troubleshooting Common Issues

1. **Slow Installation**
    - Use a stable internet connection for downloading components.
    - Avoid running other resource-intensive applications during setup.
2. **Emulator Fails to Launch**

- Ensure **Virtualization Technology (VT-x)** is enabled in your computer's BIOS.
- Allocate more RAM to the emulator in the AVD (Android Virtual Device) settings.

Hands-On Exercise: Verifying Kotlin Support

Let's ensure **Kotlin** is configured properly in Android Studio.

1. Open the newly created project.
2. Navigate to the `MainActivity.kt` file.

Replace the default code with this simple snippet:
Kotlin

```
package com.example.hellogame
```

```
import android.os.Bundle

import androidx.appcompat.app.AppCompatActivity


class MainActivity : AppCompatActivity() {

    override fun onCreate(savedInstanceState: Bundle?) {

super.onCreate(savedInstanceState)

setContentView(android.widget.TextView(this).apply {
```

```
            text = "Hello, Android Studio!"
            textSize = 24f
            textAlignment = TEXT_ALIGNMENT_CENTER
        })
    }
}
```

3.
4. Run the app on the emulator or your connected Android device. You should see the message **"Hello, Android Studio!"** displayed on the screen.

1.2 Configuring Kotlin for Android Projects

Kotlin has become the go-to programming language for Android development. It's concise, expressive, and fully supported by Google. Configuring Kotlin for your Android projects is a straightforward process since Android Studio comes with Kotlin integration out of the box. This chapter will guide you through setting up Kotlin in your projects, ensuring your environment is ready for efficient and clean development.

Why Kotlin for Android Development?

Kotlin simplifies coding by reducing boilerplate and offering features like null safety and extension functions. Plus, it's 100% interoperable with Java, allowing you to mix the two languages seamlessly.

Steps to Configure Kotlin in Your Project

Step 1: Creating a New Kotlin Project

1. **Launch Android Studio**
   Open Android Studio. On the welcome screen, click **New Project**.
2. **Select a Project Template**
   - Choose **Empty Activity** to start with a clean slate.
   - Click **Next** to proceed.
3. **Configure Your Project**
   - **Name**: Enter your project name (e.g., `MyFirstKotlinApp`).
   - **Package Name**: Customize it (e.g., `com.example.myfirstKotlinapp`).
   - **Save Location**: Select a folder on your computer.

- **Language**: Select **Kotlin** from the dropdown.
- **Minimum SDK**: Set this to **API Level 21 (Android 5.0 Lollipop)** to support a wide range of devices.
- Click **Finish**.

Note: By selecting **Kotlin** during project creation, Android Studio automatically configures your project for **Kotlin**.

Step 2: Verify Kotlin Configuration

Once your project is created, verify that **Kotlin** is correctly configured:

1. **Check Build Gradle Files**
   - Open the `build.gradle` file in the **app** module.

Ensure it includes the following dependencies:
gradle

```
plugins {
    id 'com.android.application'
    id 'org.jetbrains.kotlin.android'
}
```

o

Also, verify that the `dependencies` block includes:
gradle

```
implementation "androidx.core:core-ktx:1.12.0"
```

```
implementation
"org.jetbrains.Kotlin:Kotlin-
stdlib:1.9.10"
```

  o

2. **Sync the Project**
    o Click the **Sync Now** button that appears in the top-right corner of Android Studio to download required **Kotlin** components.

Step 3: Converting Java to Kotlin (Optional)

If you have existing Java code, you can convert it to **Kotlin** easily:

1. Open any Java file in your project.
2. Click **Code** > **Convert Java File to Kotlin File** from the menu bar.
3. Android Studio will handle the conversion for you.

Creating Your First Kotlin Function

Let's write a simple **Kotlin** function to ensure everything is working perfectly.

1. Open the `MainActivity.kt` file in the `app/src/main/java` folder.

Replace the existing code with this:
Kotlin

```
package com.example.myfirstKotlinapp


import android.os.Bundle
import android.widget.TextView
```

```kotlin
import androidx.appcompat.app.AppCompatActivity

class MainActivity : AppCompatActivity() {
    override fun onCreate(savedInstanceState: Bundle?) {
        super.onCreate(savedInstanceState)

        // Create a TextView dynamically
        val textView = TextView(this).apply {
```

```
        text = greetUser("Player")
        textSize = 20f
        textAlignment = TEXT_ALIGNMENT_CENTER
    }

    // Set the content view to the TextView
    setContentView(textView)
}

// A simple function to greet the user
```

```kotlin
fun greetUser(name: String): String {
    return "Hello, $name! Welcome to Kotlin game development!"
}
}
```

2. **Explanation of the Code**:
    - The `greetUser` function takes a `String` (name) as input and returns a greeting message.
    - The `TextView` displays this message dynamically.
    - `apply` is used to configure the `TextView` object concisely.
3. Run the app, and you'll see the message **"Hello, Player! Welcome to Kotlin game development!"** displayed.

Enhancing Your Workflow with Kotlin-Specific Tools

Kotlin Extensions (KTX)

KTX libraries simplify common tasks. For example, you can replace:

Kotlin

```
val textView = findViewById<TextView>(R.id.myTextView)
```

with:

Kotlin

```kotlin
val textView = myTextView
```

To use KTX, ensure the `core-ktx` dependency is included in your Gradle file (it usually is by default).

Null Safety in Kotlin

Kotlin's null safety prevents the dreaded `NullPointerException`. For example:

Kotlin

```kotlin
var nullableText: String? = null
// Uncommenting the next line causes a compilation error
```

```
// val length = nullableText.length
```

```
val length = nullableText?.length ?: 0  // Safe access
```

1.3 Overview of Development Tools and Resources

Building Android games requires a set of tools and resources that streamline the development process. Android Studio is your primary hub, but understanding its suite of tools and integrating external resources can elevate your productivity and creativity. In this chapter, we'll explore the development environment and essential resources to kickstart your game development journey.

Core Development Tools in Android Studio

1. Android Emulator

The Android Emulator is a virtual device that mimics an Android phone or tablet. It's perfect for testing your game without needing a physical device.

Features:

- Simulate different device configurations (screen sizes, resolutions).
- Test hardware-specific features like GPS or sensors.
- Debug with real-time logcat output.

Example Setup:

1. Open Android Studio and go to **Tools > Device Manager**.
2. Click **Create Device** and choose a hardware profile (e.g., Pixel 6).
3. Select a system image. Prefer **x86_64** for better performance.
4. Configure device settings (e.g., RAM, storage) and click **Finish**.
5. Launch the emulator by clicking the green play button.

> **Pro Tip**: Use the emulator's **Snapshot** feature to save and restore states quickly.

---

2. Layout Editor

The Layout Editor allows you to design your game's UI visually. While most games will rely on custom-rendered graphics, understanding this tool is crucial for menus, settings screens, and other non-gameplay interfaces.

Example:

1. Open `res/layout/activity_main.xml` in the **Design** view.
2. Drag and drop widgets like **Buttons**, **TextViews**, or **ImageViews** onto the canvas.
3. Adjust their properties in the **Attributes** panel.

xml

```
<TextView

android:id="@+id/gameTitle"
```

```
android:layout_width="match_p
arent"

android:layout_height="wrap_c
ontent"

    android:text="My    First
Game"

    android:textSize="24sp"

    android:gravity="center"
/>
```

3. Logcat

Logcat is Android Studio's real-time debugging console. It logs system messages, exceptions, and custom debug statements from your app.

How to Use:

Add a log statement in your code:

Kotlin

```
import android.util.Log


Log.d("MainActivity", "Game initialized successfully!")
```

1.
2. Run the app and check the **Logcat** tab in Android Studio for the message.

---

4. Profiler

The Profiler helps you monitor your app's performance. Use it to optimize your game's CPU, memory, and energy usage.

Example Use Case:

- Identify memory leaks in your game loop.
- Track frame rates to ensure smooth gameplay.

Steps:

1. Open the Profiler tab in Android Studio.
2. Run your app and start recording a session.
3. Analyze graphs to identify bottlenecks.

Essential Libraries for Game Development

1. Android Jetpack

Jetpack libraries simplify common tasks like navigation, data storage, and UI management.

Example: Use **Navigation Component** to create a main menu that transitions to the gameplay screen:

Add the dependency: gradle

```
implementation "androidx.navigation:navigation-fragment-ktx:2.7.0"

implementation "androidx.navigation:navigation-ui-ktx:2.7.0"
```

Define a navigation graph in XML: xml

```
<navigation
```

```
xmlns:android="http://schemas
.android.com/apk/res/android"

app:startDestination="@id/men
uFragment">

    <fragment

android:id="@+id/menuFragment
"

android:name="com.example.Men
uFragment" />

    <fragment

android:id="@+id/gameFragment
"
```

```
android:name="com.example.Gam
eFragment" />
</navigation>
```

2. LibGDX

LibGDX is a cross-platform game development framework that can be integrated with Android Studio.

Features:

- Advanced rendering capabilities.
- Physics and collision detection.
- Multi-platform support (Android, iOS, desktop, and web).

Resources for Graphics and Sounds

1. **Game Assets**

   - **Graphics**: Websites like OpenGameArt or Kenney Assets provide free or paid sprites, tilesets, and backgrounds.
   - **Audio**: Use freesound.org for royalty-free sound effects and background music.

   Example: Import a sprite into your project:

   1. Add the image file (`character.png`) to the `res/drawable` folder.

   Reference it in your code:
   Kotlin

```
val imageView = ImageView(this).apply {

setImageResource(R.drawable.character)
```

}

External Tools for Optimization

1. Texture Packer

Optimize your game's graphics by combining multiple textures into a single sprite sheet, reducing draw calls and improving performance.

2. Audacity

Edit and optimize audio files for your game. Ensure they are in formats compatible with Android, such as `.ogg` or `.mp3`.

Community and Learning Resources

1. Documentation and Tutorials

- [Android Developers Documentation](): The official Android development guide.
- **Kotlin** Language Reference: Learn **Kotlin** in depth.

2. Forums and Communities

- **Reddit:** Subreddits like [r/AndroidDev]() and [r/Kotlin]().
- **Stack Overflow**: Get answers to specific coding issues.

3. GitHub

Explore open-source Android game projects for inspiration and learning.

Project: Create Your First "Hello, Game!" App

In this project, we'll create a simple Android app that serves as the starting point for your game development journey. The app will display a message, "Hello, Game!" and respond to user interaction. This project will give you hands-on experience with Android Studio, **Kotlin**, and the basics of user interface (UI) design.

Step 1: Set Up the Project

1. **Create a New Project**
    - Open Android Studio and select **New Project** from the welcome screen.
    - Choose **Empty Activity** as the template and click **Next**.
2. **Configure Project Details**

- **Name:** `HelloGameApp`.
- **Package Name:** `com.example.hellogameapp`.
- **Language:** Select **Kotlin**.
- **Minimum SDK:** API Level 21 (Android 5.0 Lollipop).
- Click **Finish** to create the project.

Step 2: Design the Layout

The user interface for this app will include a text view to display the "Hello, Game!" message and a button to trigger an interaction.

1. Open the `res/layout/activity_main.xml` file in the **Design** view.
2. Add the following components to the layout:

- **TextView**: To display the greeting message.
- **Button**: To allow user interaction.

Code for `activity_main.xml`:

xml

```
<?xml version="1.0" encoding="utf-8"?>
<androidx.constraintlayout.widget.ConstraintLayout

xmlns:android="http://schemas.android.com/apk/res/android"

xmlns:app="http://schemas.android.com/apk/res-auto"
```

```xml
xmlns:tools="http://schemas.android.com/tools"

android:layout_width="match_parent"

android:layout_height="match_parent"

tools:context=".MainActivity">

    <!-- TextView for the greeting message -->
    <TextView

android:id="@+id/tvGreeting"
```

```
android:layout_width="wrap_co
ntent"

android:layout_height="wrap_c
ontent"
          android:text="Hello,
Game!"

android:textSize="24sp"

android:textStyle="bold"

android:layout_marginTop="20d
p"

android:layout_marginBottom="
20dp"
```

```
    app:layout_constraintTop_toTo
pOf="parent"

    app:layout_constraintStart_to
StartOf="parent"

    app:layout_constraintEnd_toEn
dOf="parent" />

    <!-- Button to interact
with the app -->

    <Button

android:id="@+id/btnClickMe"

android:layout_width="wrap_co
ntent"
```

```
android:layout_height="wrap_content"
        android:text="Click Me"
        app:layout_constraintTop_toBottomOf="@id/tvGreeting"
        app:layout_constraintStart_toStartOf="parent"
        app:layout_constraintEnd_toEndOf="parent" />

</androidx.constraintlayout.widget.ConstraintLayout>
```

Step 3: Add Functionality in Kotlin

Now that the layout is ready, we'll add functionality in the `MainActivity.kt` file to handle the button click and update the message dynamically.

1. Open `MainActivity.kt` from the `app/src/main/java` folder.
2. Update the code to look like this:

Code for `MainActivity.kt`:

Kotlin

```
package com.example.hellogameapp

import android.os.Bundle
import android.widget.Button
```

```kotlin
import android.widget.TextView

import androidx.appcompat.app.AppCompatActivity


class MainActivity : AppCompatActivity() {

    override fun onCreate(savedInstanceState: Bundle?) {

        super.onCreate(savedInstanceState)

        setContentView(R.layout.activity_main)
```

```kotlin
// Find views by their IDs
val tvGreeting: TextView = findViewById(R.id.tvGreeting)
val btnClickMe: Button = findViewById(R.id.btnClickMe)

// Set an onClickListener for the button
btnClickMe.setOnClickListener {
    // Update the text view with a new message
```

```
            tvGreeting.text =
"Welcome to Game Development
with Kotlin!"
        }
    }
}
```

Step 4: Run Your App

1. Connect an Android device via USB or launch the **Android Emulator**.
2. Click the **Run** button (green triangle) in Android Studio.
3. When the app launches:
    - You'll see the message **"Hello, Game!"** displayed.
    - Click the **"Click Me"** button, and the text will update to

"**Welcome to Game Development with Kotlin!**".

Step 5: Adding a Splash of Color

To make the app more visually appealing, let's style it with some colors:

Open `res/values/colors.xml` and define new colors:
xml

```
<color name="backgroundColor">#FFFAF3</color>

<color name="buttonColor">#4CAF50</color>
```

```xml
<color name="textColor">#333333</color>
```

Update the layout components: xml

```xml
<androidx.constraintlayout.widget.ConstraintLayout

    android:layout_width="match_parent"

    android:layout_height="match_parent"

    android:background="@color/backgroundColor">
```

xml

```
<TextView
```

```
android:textColor="@color/textColor" />
```

xml

```
<Button
```

```
android:backgroundTint="@color/buttonColor"
```

```
android:textColor="@android:color/white" />
```

1.

What You've Learned

By completing this project, you've:

- Created a new Android project in **Kotlin**.
- Designed a basic UI with a text view and button.
- Added interactivity to update the UI dynamically.
- Styled your app to make it visually appealing.

This "Hello, Game!" app is just the start. You're now equipped with the foundational knowledge to build more complex and interactive Android games. Let's dive deeper into game mechanics in the upcoming chapters!

Chapter 2: Kotlin Fundamentals for Game Developers

Kotlin is at the heart of Android game development. This chapter introduces you to **Kotlin**'s core concepts, equipping you with the skills to write efficient and elegant code. By the end of this chapter, you'll be familiar with variables, control flow, object-oriented programming (OOP), and handling user input—fundamental skills needed to build interactive games.

2.1 Variables, Data Types, and Control Flow

Variables, Data Types, and Control Flow

In **Kotlin**, understanding variables, data types, and control flow is essential for game development. These concepts allow you to manage data efficiently, dictate the behavior of your game, and create dynamic gameplay mechanics. Let's break down these topics step by step.

Variables in Kotlin

Variables in **Kotlin** can store data that you can use and manipulate throughout your program. **Kotlin** uses two primary keywords for declaring variables: `val` and `var`.

- `val` **(Immutable)**: Use when the value of the variable will not change.
- `var` **(Mutable)**: Use when the value may change during execution.

Example: Declaring Variables

Kotlin

```
val playerName: String = "Alex" // Immutable variable

var score: Int = 0 // Mutable variable
```

In the above example:

- `playerName` is a constant (cannot change).
- `score` can be updated as the game progresses.

Type Inference

Kotlin can infer the type of variables based on the assigned value.

Kotlin

```
val level = 1            //
Kotlin infers 'Int'

var speed = 3.5          //
Kotlin infers 'Double'
```

Data Types in Kotlin

Kotlin provides various data types that are all objects. This is especially helpful in game development for managing player attributes, game settings, and more.

Numeric Types

- **Integer types:** `Byte`, `Short`, `Int`, `Long`

- **Floating-point types**: `Float`, `Double`

Boolean

- Represents true or false values.

Character and String

- `Char`: Represents a single character.
- `String`: Represents a sequence of characters.

Example: Using Data Types

Kotlin

```
val playerLives: Int = 3

val gameSpeed: Float = 2.5f

val isGameOver: Boolean = false
```

```kotlin
val welcomeMessage: String = "Welcome to the Game!"

val initial: Char = 'A'
```

Control Flow in Kotlin

Control flow structures allow you to define the logic of your program, handle decision-making, and repeat actions.

If-Else Statements

The `if` statement executes code based on conditions.

Kotlin

```kotlin
val score = 95
```

```
if (score >= 100) {
    println("Level Up!")
} else {
    println("Keep trying!")
}
```

When Expressions

The when expression in **Kotlin** is like a switch statement but more powerful.

Kotlin

```
val difficulty = "Hard"
val message = when (difficulty) {
```

```
    "Easy"    ->    "Relax    and
enjoy!"

    "Medium"   ->   "Get   ready
for some challenge!"

    "Hard" -> "Brace yourself
for an intense experience!"

    else       ->       "Invalid
difficulty."
}
println(message)
```

Loops

- **For Loop**: Used for iterating over a range or collection.

Kotlin

```
for (i in 1..5) {
```

```
    println("Player     level: $i")
}
```

- **While Loop**: Executes as long as the condition is true.

Kotlin

```
var energy = 5
while (energy > 0) {
    println("Energy     left: $energy")
    energy--
}
```

- **Do-While Loop**: Executes at least once before checking the condition.

Kotlin

```
var attempts = 0
do {
    println("Attempt $attempts")
    attempts++
} while (attempts < 3)
```

Practical Example: Simple Game Logic

Let's create a program to track a player's progress in collecting coins.

Kotlin

```kotlin
fun main() {
    var coins = 0
    val totalCoins = 5

    while (coins < totalCoins) {
        coins++
        println("You collected a coin! Total: $coins/$totalCoins")
    }
```

```
    if (coins == totalCoins) {

println("Congratulations! You've collected all the coins.")

    }
}
```

Explanation:

- A `while` loop increases the number of coins until the total is reached.
- The `if` statement checks if the player has collected all the coins.

Output:

less

```
You collected a coin! Total:
1/5

You collected a coin! Total:
2/5

...
```

Congratulations! You've collected all the coins.

2.2 Functions, Classes, and Object-Oriented Programming

In game development, functions and object-oriented programming (OOP) are fundamental tools that allow you to organize, reuse, and structure your code effectively. They simplify complex tasks, enable modularity, and make your code easier to maintain. In this chapter, we'll dive into functions, classes, and OOP principles in **Kotlin**.

Functions in Kotlin

Functions encapsulate reusable blocks of code, making it easier to perform repetitive tasks. **Kotlin** provides a clean and concise syntax for defining functions.

Basic Function Syntax

A function in **Kotlin** starts with the `fun` keyword, followed by its name, parameters (optional), and return type.

Kotlin

```
fun greetPlayer(name: String): String {
```

```
    return "Welcome to the game, $name!"
}
```

Calling a Function

To execute the function, simply call it by its name.

Kotlin

```
val message = greetPlayer("Alex")
println(message)   // Output: Welcome to the game, Alex!
```

Functions with Default Parameters

Default parameters simplify function calls by providing a fallback value if no argument is passed.

Kotlin

```kotlin
fun startGame(difficulty: String = "Medium") {
    println("Starting game on $difficulty difficulty.")
}


startGame()                 // Uses default: Medium
startGame("Hard")           // Uses provided: Hard
```

Inline Functions

For short, single-expression functions, **Kotlin** allows you to omit curly braces and the `return` keyword.

Kotlin

```
fun square(x: Int) = x * x
println(square(4))            //
Output: 16
```

Classes in Kotlin

Classes are blueprints for creating objects, which are instances of these blueprints. They encapsulate data (properties) and behavior (functions).

Defining a Class

Here's a simple class representing a player:

Kotlin

```
class Player(val name: String, var health: Int) {

    fun displayStatus() {
        println("$name has $health health remaining.")
    }
}
```

Creating Objects

Objects are created using the `Player` class.

Kotlin

```
val player1 = Player("Alex", 100)

player1.displayStatus()    // Output: Alex has 100 health remaining.
```

Properties in Classes

You can define properties directly in the class constructor or as class members.

Kotlin

```
class GameCharacter {
    var name: String = "Unknown"
```

```kotlin
    var level: Int = 1


    fun levelUp() {
        level++
        println("$name is now level $level!")
    }
}


val hero = GameCharacter()
hero.name = "Hero"
hero.levelUp()    // Output: Hero is now level 2!
```

Object-Oriented Programming Principles

Kotlin is an object-oriented language and supports key OOP principles: encapsulation, inheritance, and polymorphism.

Encapsulation

Encapsulation involves bundling data and methods within a class and restricting access to them using visibility modifiers:

- `public`: Default, accessible everywhere.
- `private`: Accessible only within the class.
- `protected`: Accessible within the class and its subclasses.

Kotlin

```kotlin
class GameSettings {

    private var difficulty: String = "Medium"


    fun setDifficulty(level: String) {

        difficulty = level

    }


    fun showSettings() {

        println("Game difficulty is set to $difficulty.")

    }
}
```

```
val settings = GameSettings()
// settings.difficulty = "Hard" // Error: Cannot access private property
settings.setDifficulty("Hard")
settings.showSettings() // Output: Game difficulty is set to Hard.
```

Inheritance

Inheritance allows one class to acquire properties and behaviors of another class.

Kotlin

```kotlin
open class Character(val name: String) {

    fun attack() {

        println("$name attacks the enemy!")

    }
}


class Warrior(name: String) : Character(name) {

    fun defend() {

        println("$name defends against the attack!")

    }
}
```

```
val warrior = Warrior("Conan")

warrior.attack()   // Output: Conan attacks the enemy!

warrior.defend()   // Output: Conan defends against the attack!
```

Polymorphism

Polymorphism enables a single interface to represent different underlying forms. In **Kotlin**, this is achieved through method overriding.

Kotlin

```kotlin
open class Character(val name: String) {
    open fun action() {
        println("$name takes a generic action.")
    }
}


class Mage(name: String) : Character(name) {
    override fun action() {
        println("$name casts a fireball!")
    }
}
```

```
val mage = Mage("Gandalf")
mage.action()    // Output: Gandalf casts a fireball!
```

Practical Example: Game Character Manager

Let's build a simple program to manage game characters using functions, classes, and OOP principles.

Kotlin

```kotlin
open class Character(val name: String, var health: Int) {

    open fun attack() {
        println("$name attacks with basic strength!")
    }

    fun heal(amount: Int) {
        health += amount
        println("$name heals for $amount points. Health is now $health.")
    }
```

```
}


class Warrior(name: String, health: Int) : Character(name, health) {

    override fun attack() {
        println("$name swings a mighty sword!")
    }


    fun shieldBlock() {
        println("$name blocks the attack with a shield!")
    }
```

```kotlin
}


fun main() {
    val warrior = Warrior("Thor", 120)


    warrior.attack()
    // Output: Thor swings a mighty sword!

    warrior.shieldBlock()
    // Output: Thor blocks the attack with a shield!

    warrior.heal(20)
    // Output: Thor heals for 20 points. Health is now 140.

}
```

2.3 Handling User Input and Events

Handling user input and responding to events is crucial in game development. Whether it's a player tapping a button, swiping the screen, or pressing a key, games thrive on interaction. This chapter introduces you to handling user input and events in Android games using **Kotlin**. By the end, you'll know how to capture and process various types of input to make your games interactive.

Understanding User Input in Android

User input in Android can come from several sources:

- **Touch gestures** (e.g., taps, swipes, long presses)

- **Keyboard input** (e.g., pressing arrow keys or letters)
- **Sensors** (e.g., accelerometer, gyroscope)

For simplicity, we'll focus on touch gestures, as they are the most common input method for Android games.

Setting Up Touch Input

Android provides tools like **View.OnTouchListener** and **GestureDetector** to handle touch events.

Implementing Basic Touch Handling

You can attach a touch listener to any view, such as a `TextView`, `Button`, or `Canvas`.

Kotlin

```kotlin
import android.os.Bundle

import android.view.MotionEvent

import android.view.View

import androidx.appcompat.app.AppCompatActivity


class MainActivity : AppCompatActivity() {

    override fun onCreate(savedInstanceState: Bundle?) {

super.onCreate(savedInstanceState)
```

```kotlin
setContentView(R.layout.activity_main)

    val gameView: View = findViewById(R.id.game_view)



gameView.setOnTouchListener { _, event ->
    when (event.action) {

        MotionEvent.ACTION_DOWN -> {

            println("Screen touched at (${event.x}, ${event.y})")
```

                    true   // Event handled
                }

MotionEvent.ACTION_UP -> {

println("Finger lifted at (${event.x}, ${event.y})")

                    true
                }
                else -> false
            }
        }
    }
}

Explanation:

- `MotionEvent.ACTION_DOWN`: Triggered when the user touches the screen.
- `MotionEvent.ACTION_UP`: Triggered when the user lifts their finger off the screen.
- `event.x` and `event.y`: Capture the coordinates of the touch event.

Detecting Gestures with GestureDetector

For more complex gestures, such as swipes or double taps, use the `GestureDetector` class.

Example: Swipe Detection

Kotlin

```kotlin
import android.os.Bundle
import android.view.GestureDetector
import android.view.MotionEvent
import androidx.appcompat.app.AppCompatActivity


class MainActivity : AppCompatActivity(), GestureDetector.OnGestureListener {
```

```kotlin
private lateinit var gestureDetector: GestureDetector

override fun onCreate(savedInstanceState: Bundle?) {

super.onCreate(savedInstanceState)

setContentView(R.layout.activity_main)

    gestureDetector = GestureDetector(this, this)
}
```

```kotlin
    override fun onTouchEvent(event: MotionEvent): Boolean {
        return gestureDetector.onTouchEvent(event) || super.onTouchEvent(event)
    }


    override fun onDown(event: MotionEvent): Boolean {
        println("Touch down at (${event.x}, ${event.y})")
        return true
    }
```

```kotlin
    override fun onFling(e1: MotionEvent, e2: MotionEvent, velocityX: Float, velocityY: Float): Boolean {
        if (velocityX > 0) {
            println("Swipe right detected!")
        } else {
            println("Swipe left detected!")
        }
        return true
    }
```

```kotlin
    override fun onScroll(e1: MotionEvent, e2: MotionEvent, distanceX: Float, distanceY: Float): Boolean {

println("Scrolling...")
        return true
    }


    // Implement other gesture methods as needed
    override fun onShowPress(e: MotionEvent?) {}
    override fun onSingleTapUp(e: MotionEvent?): Boolean = false
```

```
    override                fun
onLongPress(e:   MotionEvent?)
{}

}
```

Key Features:

- Detects swipes using `onFling`.
- Tracks gestures like scrolling and long presses.

Handling Keyboard Input

If your game supports physical keyboards (e.g., Android TV or Chromebooks), override `onKeyDown` and `onKeyUp`.

Kotlin

```kotlin
override fun onKeyDown(keyCode: Int, event: KeyEvent): Boolean {

    when (keyCode) {

        KeyEvent.KEYCODE_DPAD_UP ->
            println("Up key pressed!")

        KeyEvent.KEYCODE_DPAD_DOWN ->
            println("Down key pressed!")

        KeyEvent.KEYCODE_SPACE ->
            println("Spacebar pressed!")

    }

    return super.onKeyDown(keyCode, event)

}
```

Key Features:

- `KeyEvent.KEYCODE_...`: Represents different keys, like arrows and letters.
- You can map specific actions (e.g., jump, attack) to key presses.

Practical Example: Moving a Sprite with Touch

Let's combine what we've learned to move a game character (sprite) based on user input.

Code Example: Move Sprite on Touch

Kotlin

```kotlin
import android.content.Context
import android.graphics.Canvas
import android.graphics.Color
import android.graphics.Paint
import android.view.MotionEvent
import android.view.View

class GameView(context: Context) : View(context) {

    private var spriteX = 100f
```

```kotlin
    private var spriteY = 100f

    private val paint = Paint().apply {
        color = Color.RED
    }


    override fun onDraw(canvas: Canvas) {
        super.onDraw(canvas)

canvas.drawCircle(spriteX, spriteY, 50f, paint)
    }
```

```kotlin
    override fun onTouchEvent(event: MotionEvent): Boolean {
        when (event.action) {
            MotionEvent.ACTION_DOWN,
            MotionEvent.ACTION_MOVE -> {
                spriteX = event.x
                spriteY = event.y
                invalidate() // Redraw the view
            }
        }
        return true
    }
```

}

Explanation:

- spriteX and spriteY: Store the sprite's position.
- onDraw: Draws the sprite at its current position.
- onTouchEvent: Updates the sprite's position when the screen is touched.

Adding the View to Activity

Kotlin

```
override                    fun
onCreate(savedInstanceState:
Bundle?) {
```

```
super.onCreate(savedInstanceS
tate)


setContentView(GameView(this)
)

}
```

Project: Build a Basic Calculator App

A calculator app is a perfect beginner project to consolidate your understanding of **Kotlin** and Android development. By building this app, you'll learn how to handle user input, work with buttons, and display results—all while practicing clean code principles.

Project Goals

1. Create a user-friendly calculator interface.
2. Perform basic operations like addition, subtraction, multiplication, and division.
3. Display results dynamically based on user input.

Step 1: Setting Up the Project

Create a New Android Project

1. Open Android Studio.
2. Select **File** > **New** > **New Project**.
3. Choose **Empty Activity** and click **Next**.
4. Name the project `BasicCalculator`.

5. Ensure **Kotlin** is selected as the language.
6. Set the **Minimum API Level** to 21 (Android 5.0) or higher.
7. Click **Finish** to generate the project.

Step 2: Designing the Layout

The layout defines the user interface. Use **LinearLayout** to align buttons and text fields vertically.

Edit `activity_main.xml`

Replace the default content with the following:

xml

```
<LinearLayout
```

```xml
xmlns:android="http://schemas.android.com/apk/res/android"

android:layout_width="match_parent"

android:layout_height="match_parent"

android:orientation="vertical"

    android:padding="16dp">

    <!-- Input Field -->

    <EditText
```

android:id="@+id/inputField"

android:layout_width="match_parent"

android:layout_height="wrap_content"

android:hint="Enter numbers and operations"

android:textSize="18sp"

android:inputType="text" />

<!-- Buttons Row 1 -->

<LinearLayout

```xml
android:layout_width="match_parent"

android:layout_height="wrap_content"

android:orientation="horizontal">

    <Button

android:id="@+id/btnAdd"

android:layout_width="0dp"

android:layout_height="wrap_content"
```

```
        android:layout_weight="1"
                    android:text="+"
/>


            <Button

android:id="@+id/btnSubtract"

android:layout_width="0dp"

android:layout_height="wrap_content"

android:layout_weight="1"
                    android:text="-"
/>
```

```xml
</LinearLayout>

<!-- Buttons Row 2 -->

<LinearLayout

android:layout_width="match_parent"

android:layout_height="wrap_content"

android:orientation="horizontal">

    <Button

android:id="@+id/btnMultiply"
```

```
            android:layout_width="0dp"

            android:layout_height="wrap_c
ontent"

            android:layout_weight="1"
            android:text="x"
/>

        <Button

            android:id="@+id/btnDivide"

            android:layout_width="0dp"
```

```
android:layout_height="wrap_c
ontent"

android:layout_weight="1"
            android:text="÷"
/>

    </LinearLayout>


    <!-- Calculate Button -->

    <Button

android:id="@+id/btnCalculate
"

android:layout_width="match_p
arent"
```

```xml
android:layout_height="wrap_content"

android:text="Calculate"

android:textSize="18sp" />

    <!-- Result Display -->
    <TextView

android:id="@+id/resultView"

android:layout_width="match_parent"
```

```
    android:layout_height="wrap_c
ontent"
        android:text="Result:
"

android:textSize="18sp"

android:paddingTop="16dp" />
```

`</LinearLayout>`

Explanation:

- **EditText**: For user input.
- **Buttons**: For operators and calculations.
- **TextView**: To display results.

Step 3: Adding Functionality

Write the logic for the calculator in `MainActivity.kt`.

Edit `MainActivity.kt`

Kotlin

```
import android.os.Bundle
import android.widget.Button
import android.widget.EditText
import android.widget.TextView
import androidx.appcompat.app.AppCompatActivity
```

```kotlin
class MainActivity : AppCompatActivity() {

    private lateinit var inputField: EditText
    private lateinit var resultView: TextView
    private var operator: String = ""
    private var number1: Double? = null

    override fun onCreate(savedInstanceState: Bundle?) {
```

```
super.onCreate(savedInstanceS
tate)

setContentView(R.layout.activ
ity_main)


    inputField             =
findViewById(R.id.inputField)
    resultView             =
findViewById(R.id.resultView)


    val btnAdd: Button  =
findViewById(R.id.btnAdd)
    val      btnSubtract:
Button                  =
findViewById(R.id.btnSubtract
)
```

```kotlin
        val btnMultiply: Button = findViewById(R.id.btnMultiply)
        val btnDivide: Button = findViewById(R.id.btnDivide)
        val btnCalculate: Button = findViewById(R.id.btnCalculate)


btnAdd.setOnClickListener { setOperator("+") }

btnSubtract.setOnClickListener { setOperator("-") }
```

```kotlin
btnMultiply.setOnClickListener { setOperator("*") }

btnDivide.setOnClickListener { setOperator("/") }

btnCalculate.setOnClickListener { calculateResult() }
}

private fun setOperator(op: String) {
    operator = op
    number1 = inputField.text.toString().toDoubleOrNull()
```

```
inputField.text.clear()    // 
Clear input for the second 
number
    }


    private                fun 
calculateResult() {
        val    number2    = 
inputField.text.toString().to
DoubleOrNull()


        if (number1 == null 
|| number2 == null) {
            resultView.text = 
"Result: Invalid Input"
            return
```

}

val result = when (operator) {

"+" -> number1!! + number2

"-" -> number1!! - number2

"*" -> number1!! * number2

"/" -> {

if (number2 == 0.0) {

resultView.text = "Result: Cannot divide by zero"

return

```
            }
                number1!!    / number2
            }
            else -> {

resultView.text = "Result: No operator selected"
                return
            }
        }
        resultView.text    = "Result: $result"
    }
}
```

Explanation:

1. **Set Operator**: Captures the first number and operator.
2. **Calculate Result**: Computes the result based on the selected operator and displays it.
3. **Validation**: Handles invalid input and division by zero gracefully.

Step 4: Testing the Calculator

Run the app:

- Enter two numbers separated by an operator (e.g., 5 and 3).
- Tap an operator button (+, -, ×, ÷).
- Tap **Calculate** to see the result.

This chapter introduced **Kotlin**'s core concepts, covering variables, control flow, functions, and classes. By completing the calculator app, you've reinforced these concepts with practical application—preparing you to tackle game logic in the upcoming chapters!

Chapter 3: Understanding the Android Framework

The Android Framework is the backbone of Android development. It provides the tools and structure needed to build responsive, interactive apps. For game development, understanding key components like Activities, Fragments, the Android Lifecycle, and layouts is essential. This chapter introduces these concepts and demonstrates how to use them effectively.

3.1 Activities, Fragments, and the Android Lifecycle

In Android development, **Activities** and **Fragments** are the core components that manage the user interface (UI) and user interaction. Understanding how they work and how their lifecycle functions is crucial to creating efficient, responsive apps.

Activities

An **Activity** in Android represents a single screen with which the user can interact. Each Activity is a different screen or UI component of your app. It's the entry point for an app and manages user input, performs operations, and provides output to the user.

Activity Lifecycle

The Android operating system runs your app's Activities within a set of predefined lifecycle stages. Each stage triggers specific methods that help you manage your app's resources. Let's look at the most important lifecycle methods for an Activity:

`onCreate()`: This method is called when the Activity is first created. It's where you'll typically set up your layout with `setContentView()` and initialize components.

Example:
Kotlin

```
override fun onCreate(savedInstanceState: Bundle?) {

    super.onCreate(savedInstanceState)

    setContentView(R.layout.activity_main)

}
```

- `onStart()`: Called when the Activity becomes visible to the user, but not yet interactive.

- `onResume()`: The Activity is now interactive. This is where you'll want to start animations, begin listening to user input, or restart any services that were paused.
- `onPause()`: This method is called when the user navigates away from the Activity, but it's still visible. Here, you should release resources that you don't need while the Activity is paused.
- `onStop()`: The Activity is no longer visible to the user. This is a good place to save data or stop processes like background services.
- `onDestroy()`: Called just before the Activity is destroyed. You should use this method to clean up any resources that need to be released before the Activity is destroyed.

Here's a simple example of an Activity lifecycle in **Kotlin**:

Kotlin

```
class MainActivity : AppCompatActivity() {

    override fun onCreate(savedInstanceState: Bundle?) {

super.onCreate(savedInstanceState)
        Log.d("Lifecycle", "onCreate called")
```

```
setContentView(R.layout.activity_main)
    }


    override fun onStart() {
        super.onStart()
        Log.d("Lifecycle", "onStart called")
    }


    override fun onResume() {
        super.onResume()
        Log.d("Lifecycle", "onResume called")
```

}

```
override fun onPause() {

    super.onPause()

    Log.d("Lifecycle", "onPause called")

}


override fun onStop() {

    super.onStop()

    Log.d("Lifecycle", "onStop called")

}
```

```
    override fun onDestroy()
{
        super.onDestroy()
        Log.d("Lifecycle", "onDestroy called")
    }
}
```

By understanding how the lifecycle works, you can make your app more efficient, saving resources when necessary and ensuring that the user's experience remains smooth.

Fragments

Fragments are like **mini-Activities**. They are modular sections of an Activity's user interface. You can think of fragments as reusable pieces of UI that can be combined in different ways within an Activity. One Activity can host several fragments.

Fragment Lifecycle

Fragments also have their own lifecycle, which is similar to Activities but tailored to the modular nature of fragments. Here are the key lifecycle methods for fragments:

- `onAttach()`: Called when the fragment is associated with an activity.
- `onCreateView()`: This is where you inflate the layout of the fragment, essentially creating the fragment's user interface.
- `onActivityCreated()`: Called when the Activity's `onCreate()` method has completed. At this point, the fragment is fully initialized.
- `onStart()`: The fragment becomes visible to the user.

- `onResume()`: The fragment starts interacting with the user.
- `onPause()`: The fragment is no longer interacting with the user.
- `onStop()`: The fragment is no longer visible.
- `onDestroyView()`: The view associated with the fragment is being removed.
- `onDetach()`: The fragment is no longer attached to its parent activity.

Here's a simple example of a Fragment lifecycle in **Kotlin**:

Kotlin

```
class     ExampleFragment     :
Fragment() {
```

```kotlin
override fun onAttach(context: Context) {

super.onAttach(context)

Log.d("FragmentLifecycle", "onAttach called")

}


override fun onCreateView(

    inflater: LayoutInflater, container: ViewGroup?,

    savedInstanceState: Bundle?

): View? {
```

```kotlin
        Log.d("FragmentLifecycle", "onCreateView called")
        return inflater.inflate(R.layout.fragment_example, container, false)
    }

    override fun onStart() {
        super.onStart()
        Log.d("FragmentLifecycle", "onStart called")
    }

    override fun onResume() {
```

```kotlin
        super.onResume()

    Log.d("FragmentLifecycle", "onResume called")
        }


        override fun onPause() {
            super.onPause()

    Log.d("FragmentLifecycle", "onPause called")
        }


        override fun onStop() {
            super.onStop()
```

```kotlin
        Log.d("FragmentLifecycle", "onStop called")
    }

    override fun onDestroyView() {
        super.onDestroyView()

        Log.d("FragmentLifecycle", "onDestroyView called")
    }

    override fun onDetach() {
        super.onDetach()
```

```
Log.d("FragmentLifecycle",
"onDetach called")

    }
}
```

Managing Activities and Fragments

Understanding how activities and fragments interact is key when designing Android applications. Activities serve as the container for fragments and allow you to create dynamic UIs. Fragments help you break down the UI into manageable pieces, making your app modular and more maintainable.

Practical Example: Activity and Fragment Interaction

Let's create a simple app where a fragment is added to an Activity. We'll also make sure that the Activity and Fragment interact with each other by passing data.

1. **MainActivity** - Hosts the Fragment.
2. **ExampleFragment** - Displays a button, and when clicked, it communicates back to the Activity.

Kotlin

```
// MainActivity.kt
class MainActivity : AppCompatActivity(), ExampleFragment.OnButtonClickListener {

    override fun onCreate(savedInstanceState: Bundle?) {
```

```
super.onCreate(savedInstanceS
tate)

setContentView(R.layout.activ
ity_main)

        if
(savedInstanceState == null)
{
            //    Add    the
fragment to the activity
            val  fragment   =
ExampleFragment()

supportFragmentManager.beginT
ransaction()
```

```
            .add(R.id.fragment_container, fragment)
                    .commit()
        }
    }


    override fun onButtonClick(message: String) {
        // Handle the button click event from the fragment
        Toast.makeText(this, message, Toast.LENGTH_SHORT).show()
    }
}
```

```kotlin
// ExampleFragment.kt
class    ExampleFragment    : Fragment() {

    interface OnButtonClickListener {
        fun onButtonClick(message: String)
    }

    var         listener: OnButtonClickListener? = null
```

```kotlin
override fun onAttach(context: Context) {

super.onAttach(context)
    listener = context as? OnButtonClickListener

}


override fun onCreateView(
    inflater: LayoutInflater, container: ViewGroup?,
    savedInstanceState: Bundle?
): View? {
```

```kotlin
        val rootView = inflater.inflate(R.layout.fragment_example, container, false)

        val button: Button = rootView.findViewById(R.id.button)

button.setOnClickListener {

listener?.onButtonClick("Button clicked in fragment")

        }
        return rootView
    }


    override fun onDetach() {
```

```
        super.onDetach()

        listener = null

    }
}
```

In this example, we've set up communication between an Activity and a Fragment. When the button in the fragment is clicked, it triggers the `onButtonClick()` method in the MainActivity, which displays a `Toast` message.

3.2 Creating and Managing Layouts for Games

When building Android games, one of the most crucial aspects is creating layouts that not only look great but also enhance user interaction and performance. Layouts define the appearance of your game's UI components and determine how players interact with your game. In this chapter, we'll explore how to effectively create and manage layouts for games in Android using XML and **Kotlin**, ensuring the layouts are both functional and efficient.

Understanding Layouts in Android

Android provides a flexible system for creating layouts using XML. In games, layouts often need to be simple and efficient, as the main focus is usually on the gameplay itself. That said, you still need to create a user interface (UI) that can display important game data, such as scores, timers, and buttons for game controls.

Android Layout Types

There are several types of layouts in Android, but for games, we often use:

- **FrameLayout**: A basic layout for stacking views on top of each other. It is typically used for simple UIs where the content overlaps.
- **RelativeLayout**: Allows you to position elements relative to one another. This is useful when you want to place a UI element (like a score counter) at the top-left of the screen, for example.
- **LinearLayout**: Arranges views in a single column or row. While useful for simple layouts, it might not be ideal for game UIs because it can be restrictive.
- **ConstraintLayout**: The most flexible and powerful layout, allowing for precise control over the positioning of UI components. This is the recommended layout for complex game interfaces.

For games, we often use **FrameLayout** and **ConstraintLayout** to ensure that the game's primary content (e.g., game board or sprite) is easily manageable without interfering with UI elements.

Step 1: Designing the Game Layout in XML

Let's start by designing a basic layout for a simple game. In this example, we'll create a layout with a game area (such as a canvas), a score display, and a start button.

We'll use **ConstraintLayout** to position these elements efficiently.

Here's how the `activity_game.xml` layout might look:

xml

```xml
<?xml version="1.0" encoding="utf-8"?>
<androidx.constraintlayout.widget.ConstraintLayout
    xmlns:android="http://schemas.android.com/apk/res/android"
    xmlns:app="http://schemas.android.com/apk/res-auto"
    xmlns:tools="http://schemas.android.com/tools"
    android:layout_width="match_parent"
    android:layout_height="match_parent"
```

```xml
    tools:context=".GameActivity"
    >



    <!-- Game area (where the game will be drawn) -->
    <FrameLayout

        android:id="@+id/gameArea"

        android:layout_width="0dp"

        android:layout_height="0dp"

        app:layout_constraintTop_toTopOf="parent"
```

```
app:layout_constraintBottom_t
oTopOf="@+id/scoreLayout"

app:layout_constraintLeft_toL
eftOf="parent"

app:layout_constraintRight_to
RightOf="parent"

android:background="@android:
color/black" />

    <!-- Score display -->
    <TextView

android:id="@+id/scoreText"
```

```
android:layout_width="wrap_co
ntent"

android:layout_height="wrap_c
ontent"

        android:text="Score:
0"

android:textSize="18sp"

app:layout_constraintTop_toBo
ttomOf="@+id/gameArea"

app:layout_constraintLeft_toL
eftOf="parent"
```

```
android:textColor="@android:color/white" />

    <!-- Start button -->
    <Button

android:id="@+id/startButton"

android:layout_width="wrap_content"

android:layout_height="wrap_content"

        android:text="Start Game"
```

```
app:layout_constraintTop_toBo
ttomOf="@+id/scoreText"

app:layout_constraintLeft_toL
eftOf="parent"

app:layout_constraintRight_to
RightOf="parent"

android:layout_marginTop="16d
p" />
</androidx.constraintlayout.w
idget.ConstraintLayout>
```

Explanation of XML Layout:

- **FrameLayout (Game Area)**: This is where your game's main content will be displayed (like a canvas or game board). We've set it to match the width of the parent and adjusted its height to be dynamic based on the size of the score display below.
- **TextView (Score Display)**: A simple text element to show the player's score. It is positioned below the game area and above the start button.
- **Button (Start Game)**: The start button to begin the game. It's placed below the score display and centered horizontally.

Step 2: Handling the Game Area with Kotlin

Now that we have designed the layout, let's move to the **Kotlin** side of things to handle interactions and game mechanics. First, we will set up the `GameActivity` class to link the layout with code and manage the start button.

Kotlin

```kotlin
class GameActivity : AppCompatActivity() {

    private lateinit var gameArea: FrameLayout

    private lateinit var scoreText: TextView

    private lateinit var startButton: Button

    private var score = 0


    override fun onCreate(savedInstanceState: Bundle?) {
```

```
super.onCreate(savedInstanceS
tate)

setContentView(R.layout.activ
ity_game)

        // Bind views
        gameArea                =
findViewById(R.id.gameArea)
        scoreText               =
findViewById(R.id.scoreText)
        startButton             =
findViewById(R.id.startButton
)
```

```
    // Handle the start button click

startButton.setOnClickListener {
        startGame()
    }
}


    // Start the game and initialize score
    private fun startGame() {
        score = 0
        updateScoreDisplay()
```

```
        // Initialize or reset game area (such as clearing the canvas)
        gameArea.removeAllViews()

        // You can add game logic here, such as creating game objects or starting a timer
    }

    // Update the score display
    private fun updateScoreDisplay() {
```

```
        scoreText.text        =
"Score: $score"

    }

}
```

Explanation of Kotlin Code:

- **Binding Views:** We use `findViewById()` to link the XML layout components (like `gameArea`, `scoreText`, and `startButton`) to the **Kotlin** code.
- **Button Click Listener**: When the "Start Game" button is clicked, the `startGame()` method is called to initialize the game, reset the score, and clear the game area.
- **Updating the Score**: The score is updated using the `updateScoreDisplay()`

method, which modifies the `TextView` to display the current score.

Step 3: Dynamic Content Creation

Now that you have the basic layout, you can begin adding more dynamic elements to the game area. For instance, if you're making a shooting game, you might add objects (like enemy ships or bullets) into the `gameArea` using **Canvas** or **SurfaceView**. These elements can be drawn and updated dynamically, providing real-time game feedback.

Here's how you could add a simple drawing element, like a circle, on the `FrameLayout`:

Kotlin

```kotlin
class GameActivity : AppCompatActivity() {

    private lateinit var gameArea: FrameLayout
    private lateinit var scoreText: TextView
    private lateinit var startButton: Button
    private var score = 0

    override fun onCreate(savedInstanceState: Bundle?) {

super.onCreate(savedInstanceS
tate)
```

```
setContentView(R.layout.activity_game)

        // Bind views
        gameArea      = findViewById(R.id.gameArea)
        scoreText     = findViewById(R.id.scoreText)
        startButton   = findViewById(R.id.startButton)

        // Handle the start button click
```

```
startButton.setOnClickListene
r {

            startGame()

        }

    }


    private fun startGame() {

        score = 0

        updateScoreDisplay()


gameArea.removeAllViews()


        // Draw a simple
circle on the game area
```

```kotlin
        val circleView = CircleView(this)

gameArea.addView(circleView)
    }


    private fun updateScoreDisplay() {
        scoreText.text = "Score: $score"
    }
}


// Custom view to draw a circle
```

```kotlin
class CircleView(context: Context) : View(context) {
    override fun onDraw(canvas: Canvas) {
        super.onDraw(canvas)
        val paint = Paint()
        paint.color = Color.RED
        paint.style = Paint.Style.FILL

canvas.drawCircle(150f, 150f, 50f, paint) // Draw a circle at position (150, 150)
    }
}
```

In this code:

- **CircleView**: We create a custom `View` class that draws a circle on the canvas. The circle is drawn at a fixed position with a radius of 50 pixels.
- **Adding Circle to the Game Area**: When the game starts, a new `CircleView` is created and added to the `gameArea`.

3.3 Basics of XML and Views in Android

When it comes to Android development, XML (Extensible Markup Language) plays a crucial role in defining the user interface (UI). Understanding how to use XML to design layouts and handle different types of views is essential for creating engaging and interactive Android games. In this chapter, we'll explore the basics of XML and how to use various views in Android to build functional game interfaces.

What is XML in Android?

XML is a markup language used to define the structure and appearance of a UI in Android applications. It's used to describe the layout of a screen, including buttons, text fields, images, and other UI elements. Android uses XML to separate the visual structure from the business logic, which means you can focus on designing the interface while keeping your **Kotlin** code clean and maintainable.

Android Views and View Groups

In Android, **Views** are the building blocks of the user interface. A **View** represents a UI element, such as a button, text box, image, or even a game object like a sprite. A **ViewGroup** is a container that holds and arranges Views within itself. Examples of ViewGroups include `LinearLayout`, `FrameLayout`, and `ConstraintLayout`, which we discussed earlier.

Let's break down the most commonly used views and their attributes.

Commonly Used Views

TextView: Displays text on the screen. It's used for showing information, such as scores, timers, or game instructions. Example:
xml

```
<TextView

android:id="@+id/scoreText"

android:layout_width="wrap_content"
```

```
        android:layout_height="wrap_c
ontent"
            android:text="Score: 0"
            android:textSize="18sp"

android:textColor="@android:c
olor/white"

app:layout_constraintTop_toTo
pOf="parent"

app:layout_constraintLeft_toL
eftOf="parent" />
```

1. **Explanation**:
    - The `TextView` displays the player's score. We use the `android:text` attribute to set the text, and the `android:textColor` and `android:textSize`

- attributes to define the text color and size.
  - The `layout_constraintTop_toTopOf` and `layout_constraintLeft_toLeftOf` are used to position the text relative to the parent layout using `ConstraintLayout`.

Button: A clickable element used for user interaction. In games, buttons are commonly used for starting the game, pausing, or controlling game actions. Example:
xml

```
<Button

android:id="@+id/startButton"
```

```
    android:layout_width="wrap_co
ntent"

    android:layout_height="wrap_c
ontent"
        android:text="Start Game"

    android:textColor="@android:c
olor/white"

    app:layout_constraintTop_toBo
ttomOf="@+id/scoreText"

    app:layout_constraintLeft_toL
eftOf="parent" />
```

2. **Explanation**:
   - This button has the label "Start Game" and is linked to the `scoreText` view to position it below the score. The button will

be used to trigger game-related actions when clicked.

ImageView: Displays images, such as game sprites or backgrounds. You will use this to display game objects or icons within your game.
Example:
xml

```
<ImageView

android:id="@+id/playerSprite"

android:layout_width="wrap_content"

android:layout_height="wrap_content"
```

```
android:src="@drawable/player
_icon"

app:layout_constraintTop_toTo
pOf="parent"

app:layout_constraintLeft_toL
eftOf="parent" />
```

3. **Explanation**:
    - The `ImageView` displays an image (`@drawable/player_icon`) that represents the player's character in the game. This view can be dynamically updated during the game, such as moving the character or changing its state.

ProgressBar: Often used to show the progress of a task, like loading, health bar, or game timer.

Example:

xml

```xml
<ProgressBar

android:id="@+id/healthBar"

android:layout_width="wrap_content"

android:layout_height="wrap_content"
    android:progress="50"
    android:max="100"

android:layout_marginTop="20dp"

app:layout_constraintTop_toBottomOf="@+id/startButton"
```

```
app:layout_constraintLeft_toL
eftOf="parent" />
```

4. **Explanation**:
    - This `ProgressBar` displays the player's health in a game, with a progress value that can be updated as the game progresses. The `android:progress` attribute defines the current progress, and the `android:max` attribute defines the maximum value (100%).

How to Use Views in Your Game

Once you have defined your UI components in XML, you need to interact with them in your **Kotlin** code. Android provides a simple way to find and manipulate views using `findViewById` and event listeners like `setOnClickListener`.

Here's how you can interact with the views defined in the XML layout:

Kotlin

```
class GameActivity : AppCompatActivity() {

    private lateinit var scoreText: TextView
    private lateinit var startButton: Button
    private lateinit var playerSprite: ImageView
    private lateinit var healthBar: ProgressBar
    private var score = 0
```

```kotlin
override fun onCreate(savedInstanceState: Bundle?) {

    super.onCreate(savedInstanceState)

    setContentView(R.layout.activity_game)

    // Bind views
    scoreText = findViewById(R.id.scoreText)
    startButton = findViewById(R.id.startButton)
    playerSprite = findViewById(R.id.playerSprite)
    healthBar = findViewById(R.id.healthBar)
```

```kotlin
        // Set the start button click listener
startButton.setOnClickListener {
            startGame()
        }
    }

    private fun startGame() {
        score = 0
        updateScoreDisplay()
        healthBar.progress = 100 // Reset health bar
        // Add logic to start the game, such as setting up game objects, enemies, etc.
    }

    private fun updateScoreDisplay() {
```

```
        scoreText.text =
"Score: $score"
    }
}
```

Explanation of the Kotlin Code:

- **Binding Views**: We use `findViewById()` to link the UI components (such as `scoreText`, `startButton`, and `healthBar`) defined in the XML layout to the **Kotlin** code.
- **Button Click Listener**: When the "Start Game" button is clicked, the `startGame()` function is called to reset the score and health bar, and to initiate the game logic.
- **Updating the Score**: The `updateScoreDisplay()` method

updates the `TextView` that shows the player's score.

Views and Performance

When building Android games, it's important to balance the use of views for UI elements with performance. Too many complex views on the screen can cause performance issues, especially when dealing with graphics-heavy games. Here are some tips to keep performance in check:

- Use `FrameLayout` or `SurfaceView` for rendering game graphics.
- Avoid nesting too many views, as it can increase layout complexity and slow down rendering.
- Update views only when necessary to avoid redundant processing.

Project: Design a Simple App Layout with Interactive Buttons

In this hands-on project, we'll design a simple Android app with a layout that includes interactive buttons. This project is aimed at beginners, but also serves as a quick refresher for more experienced developers. You'll learn how to create a basic UI layout using XML, connect UI elements in **Kotlin**, and handle button click events.

By the end of this chapter, you will have a working app where the user can interact with buttons to change the displayed text. Let's jump right in!

What You'll Need

Before we begin, ensure that you have:

- **Android Studio** installed on your computer (as detailed in previous chapters).

- A **basic understanding of Kotlin** and how Android apps are structured.

Step 1: Create a New Android Project

1. Open **Android Studio**.
2. Select **Start a new Android Studio project**.
3. Choose the **Empty Activity** template.
4. Name your project: `InteractiveButtonApp`.
5. Set the language to **Kotlin**.
6. Choose the appropriate API level (we'll use **API 21** or higher for this project).
7. Click **Finish** to create the project.

Android Studio will set up the project, creating necessary files like `MainActivity.kt` and `activity_main.xml`.

Step 2: Designing the Layout with XML

The layout of our app will consist of the following UI components:

- A **TextView** to display the message.
- Two **Buttons**: one to change the message and one to reset it.

Let's now open the `activity_main.xml` file and design the layout.

1. **Navigate to** `res > layout > activity_main.xml`.
2. Replace the existing XML code with the following layout design:

xml

```
<?xml version="1.0" encoding="utf-8"?>
<androidx.constraintlayout.widget.ConstraintLayout
xmlns:android="http://schemas.android.com/apk/res/android"

xmlns:app="http://schemas.android.com/apk/res-auto"
```

xmlns:tools="http://schemas.android.com/tools"

android:layout_width="match_parent"

android:layout_height="match_parent"

tools:context=".MainActivity">

    <!-- TextView to display the message -->
    <TextView

android:id="@+id/textView"

android:layout_width="wrap_content"

```xml
android:layout_height="wrap_content"
        android:text="Hello, Android!"
    android:textSize="24sp"
    android:textColor="@android:color/black"
    app:layout_constraintTop_toTopOf="parent"
    app:layout_constraintLeft_toLeftOf="parent"
    app:layout_constraintRight_toRightOf="parent"
    app:layout_constraintBottom_toTopOf="@+id/buttonChange" />
```

```xml
<!-- Button to change the text -->
    <Button
        android:id="@+id/buttonChange"
        android:layout_width="wrap_content"
        android:layout_height="wrap_content"
        android:text="Change Text"
        android:textSize="18sp"
        app:layout_constraintTop_toBottomOf="@+id/textView"
```

```xml
        app:layout_constraintLeft_toLeftOf="parent"

        app:layout_constraintRight_toRightOf="parent"

        android:layout_marginTop="20dp" />

    <!-- Button to reset the text -->
    <Button
        android:id="@+id/buttonReset"
        android:layout_width="wrap_content"
        android:layout_height="wrap_content"
```

```
        android:text="Reset Text"

android:textSize="18sp"

app:layout_constraintTop_toBottomOf="@+id/buttonChange"

app:layout_constraintLeft_toLeftOf="parent"

app:layout_constraintRight_toRightOf="parent"

android:layout_marginTop="20dp" />

</androidx.constraintlayout.widget.ConstraintLayout>
```

Explanation of the XML Layout:

- **ConstraintLayout**: The `ConstraintLayout` is the root layout, allowing us to easily position elements relative to each other and the parent layout.
- **TextView**: Displays the initial message "Hello, Android!" in large, black text. It is centered at the top of the screen.
- **Buttons**: There are two buttons:
    - **Change Text**: Will change the text in the `TextView`.
    - **Reset Text**: Will reset the text back to "Hello, Android!"

Step 3: Writing the Kotlin Code

Now that we've designed the layout, we need to handle the logic behind the buttons. Let's open `MainActivity.kt` and implement the functionality.

1. **Navigate to** `MainActivity.kt` (located in `src > main > java > com.example.interactivebuttonapp`).
2. Replace the existing code with the following:

Kotlin

```
package com.example.interactivebuttonapp

import android.os.Bundle
import android.widget.Button
import android.widget.TextView
import androidx.appcompat.app.AppCompatActivity
```

```kotlin
class MainActivity : AppCompatActivity() {

    // Declare the views
    private lateinit var textView: TextView
    private lateinit var buttonChange: Button
    private lateinit var buttonReset: Button

    override fun onCreate(savedInstanceState: Bundle?) {

        super.onCreate(savedInstanceState)

        setContentView(R.layout.activity_main)
```

```
        // Bind views to
their respective UI elements
        textView                =
findViewById(R.id.textView)
        buttonChange            =
findViewById(R.id.buttonChang
e)
        buttonReset             =
findViewById(R.id.buttonReset
)

        // Set up the
onClickListener for the
Change Text button
        buttonChange.setOnClickListen
er {
            changeText()
        }
```

```
    // Set up the 
onClickListener for the Reset 
Text button

buttonReset.setOnClickListene
r {
            resetText()
        }
    }


    // Function to change the 
text in the TextView
    private fun changeText() 
{
        textView.text = "Text 
Changed! Enjoy your app."
    }

    // Function to reset the 
text in the TextView
    private fun resetText() {
```

```
        textView.text         = "Hello, Android!"
    }
}
```

Explanation of the Kotlin Code:

- **Binding Views**:
    - We use `findViewById()` to get references to the `TextView` and `Button` UI elements from the layout (`activity_main.xml`).
    - `textView`, `buttonChange`, and `buttonReset` are variables that will hold the references to these UI components.
- **Button Listeners**:
    - We use `setOnClickListener()`

for both buttons to respond to click events.
- When the **Change Text** button is clicked, the `changeText()` function is called, which changes the text in the `TextView` to "Text Changed! Enjoy your app."
- When the **Reset Text** button is clicked, the `resetText()` function is called, resetting the text back to "Hello, Android!".

Step 4: Running the App

1. **Connect your Android device** to your computer or use the **Android Emulator**.
2. In Android Studio, click the green **Run** button (or use `Shift + F10`) to launch the app on your device or emulator.
3. When the app starts, you'll see the text "Hello, Android!" displayed.

4. Click the **Change Text** button, and the message will change to "Text Changed! Enjoy your app."
5. Click the **Reset Text** button, and the message will revert to "Hello, Android!"

Recap

In this project, you've learned how to:

- Design a simple layout with XML.
- Bind UI components (like `TextView` and `Button`) to **Kotlin** code.
- Handle button click events with `setOnClickListener()`.
- Dynamically update the UI (e.g., changing text in a `TextView`) based on user interactions.

This project serves as a great foundation for understanding how to create interactive UI elements in Android. By building on this knowledge, you'll be able to implement more advanced features and design sophisticated user interfaces for your Android games.

Part 2:
Game Design Fundamentals

Chapter 4: Introduction to Game Design

In this chapter, we will take a step back from coding and dive into the creative side of Android game development: **Game Design**. This is a crucial step for building any game, as it sets the foundation for everything from gameplay mechanics to visual style. By understanding the core concepts of game design, you'll be able to create engaging, fun, and meaningful experiences for your players.

We'll break down the essentials of game mechanics, explore how sprites and animation work, touch on the basics of game physics, and wrap up with a hands-on project where you'll storyboard a simple game idea. By the end of this chapter, you'll have a clearer picture of what goes into designing a game.

4.1 Key Elements of Game Mechanics

Game mechanics are the foundational rules and systems that drive player interactions within a game. They define how the game operates, how players engage with the environment, and how the game challenges players. To make a game enjoyable and engaging, understanding game mechanics is crucial—whether you're designing a simple puzzle game or a complex action-packed platformer. In this chapter, we'll break down the key elements that make up game mechanics, along with practical examples to help you grasp the concepts.

What Are Game Mechanics?

Game mechanics are the building blocks of gameplay. They involve everything that governs player actions and the game world's response to those actions. These mechanics are essential because they dictate how players move, interact with objects, and experience progression. Every game, from a simple mobile puzzle game to a fully immersive 3D RPG, has its unique set of mechanics.

Game mechanics can be categorized into different types, but the main ones you will work with in game development include **movement, combat, collection, puzzles**, and **progression**. Let's go through each of these mechanics in detail.

---

1. Movement Mechanics

Movement is one of the most fundamental mechanics in almost every game. It refers to how players control their characters or objects within the game world. Understanding how to create smooth, responsive movement is key to engaging gameplay.

Types of Movement Mechanics:

- **Linear Movement**: Characters move in a straight line from one point to another.
- **Platformer Movement**: Characters move in two or three dimensions, often involving jumping, walking, and climbing platforms.
- **Exploration Movement**: Games with large worlds, like RPGs, often include free-roaming mechanics where the player can explore vast environments.

Example: Simple Platformer Movement

In a 2D platformer, the character usually has the ability to move left and right and jump. Let's say the player presses the right arrow key to move the character to the right and presses the space bar to make the character jump.

Here's an example of simple movement code for a 2D game in **Kotlin**:

Kotlin

```kotlin
// Kotlin code for basic movement in a 2D game

var playerX = 0f // Player's X position

var playerY = 0f // Player's Y position

var speed = 5f // Movement speed


fun updatePlayerMovement() {
```

```
    if (isKeyPressed(KeyEvent.KEYCODE_RIGHT)) {
        playerX += speed // Move player to the right
    }
    if (isKeyPressed(KeyEvent.KEYCODE_LEFT)) {
        playerX -= speed // Move player to the left
    }
    if (isKeyPressed(KeyEvent.KEYCODE_SPACE)) {
        jump() // Call a function to make the player jump
```

```
    }
}


// Function to make the player jump
fun jump() {
    // Implement jumping mechanics, such as applying gravity
    playerY -= 10f // Jump upward
}
```

In this code, `isKeyPressed` checks whether the right or left arrow key or space bar is pressed, and moves the player accordingly.

The jump function moves the player upward when the space bar is pressed.

---

2. Combat Mechanics

Combat mechanics are essential in many games, especially action or adventure genres. These mechanics govern how players attack, defend, and interact with enemies or obstacles within the game.

Types of Combat Mechanics:

- **Melee Combat:** Close-range combat, like swinging a sword or punching.
- **Ranged Combat**: Long-range combat, such as shooting arrows, bullets, or magic.
- **Defensive Mechanics**: Includes blocking, dodging, or using shields to protect the player from damage.

Example: Simple Shooting Mechanic

Let's consider a simple shooting mechanic for a game. The player might have a gun, and the goal is to shoot projectiles at enemies. Here's a code snippet in **Kotlin** for shooting a projectile:

Kotlin

```
var bulletSpeed = 10f // Speed of the bullet
var bullets = mutableListOf<Bullet>() // List to store bullets


// Bullet class to define the properties of the bullet
```

```kotlin
class Bullet(var x: Float, var y: Float, val speed: Float) {
    fun move() {
        x += speed // Move the bullet horizontally
    }
}


// Shooting function
fun shootBullet(playerX: Float, playerY: Float) {
    // Create a new bullet when the player presses a button
```

```
    val       bullet        =
Bullet(playerX,      playerY,
bulletSpeed)

    bullets.add(bullet)    //
Add the bullet to the list


    // Call move() to make
the bullet move
    for (bullet in bullets) {
        bullet.move()
    }
}
```

In this example, the Bullet class defines the position and movement of the bullet. When the player presses the shoot button, the `shootBullet` function creates a new bullet and adds it to a list of active bullets.

3. Collection Mechanics

In many games, players collect items, such as coins, power-ups, or health packs. Collection mechanics are often a key part of the game loop and can provide both challenges and rewards.

Types of Collection Mechanics:

- **Item Pickup**: Players collect items scattered throughout the game world.
- **Power-Ups**: Special items that grant temporary abilities or advantages.
- **Currency**: In many games, players collect in-game currency, such as coins, to unlock new features or levels.

Example: Collecting Coins

Here's an example of how a player might collect coins in a 2D platformer:

Kotlin

```kotlin
var playerX = 0f // Player's X position

var playerY = 0f // Player's Y position

var score = 0 // Player's score


// Coin class to represent collectible items

class Coin(var x: Float, var y: Float, var isCollected: Boolean = false)
```

```kotlin
var coins = listOf(Coin(100f, 200f), Coin(200f, 300f)) // List of coins in the game

fun checkCoinCollection() {
    for (coin in coins) {
        if (!coin.isCollected && playerX == coin.x && playerY == coin.y) {
            coin.isCollected = true // Mark the coin as collected
            score += 10 // Increase score by 10 points
        }
    }
```

}

In this code, each coin is checked to see if the player is on its position. If the player collects the coin, it is marked as collected, and the score increases.

4. Puzzle Mechanics

Puzzle mechanics challenge players to think critically, solve problems, and make strategic decisions. These mechanics often appear in adventure or strategy games.

Types of Puzzle Mechanics:

- **Logic puzzles**: Solve problems using reasoning and deduction.
- **Matching**: Games like "Match-3" (think of Candy Crush) rely on matching pieces to clear them from the board.

- **Timed Challenges**: Players are given a limited amount of time to solve a puzzle.

Example: Basic Puzzle Logic

Imagine a game where the player has to match colored blocks to progress to the next level. Here's a simple logic check:

Kotlin

```
var redBlock = false // Red block status
var blueBlock = false // Blue block status


// Function to check if the player has solved the puzzle
fun checkPuzzleSolution() {
```

```
    if     (redBlock    &&
blueBlock) {

        println("Puzzle
solved!") // Print message if
puzzle is solved

    } else {

        println("Keep
trying!")

    }

}
```

In this example, the puzzle is solved when both redBlock and blueBlock are true.

---

5. Progression Mechanics

Progression mechanics keep players engaged by offering rewards, challenges, and the opportunity to grow stronger or unlock new areas. These mechanics provide a sense of accomplishment and keep the game interesting.

Types of Progression Mechanics:

- **Leveling Up:** Increasing a character's stats, like health or strength, as the player advances.
- **Unlockables**: New abilities, areas, or features that are unlocked after completing certain tasks.
- **Story Progression**: Unlocking new story elements or plot points as players progress through the game.

Example: Leveling Up

In many RPGs, players level up by gaining experience points (XP) after defeating enemies or completing quests.

Kotlin

```kotlin
var playerLevel = 1

var playerXP = 0

val xpToLevelUp = 100


// Function to handle XP and level up
fun gainXP(xp: Int) {
    playerXP += xp
    if (playerXP >= xpToLevelUp) {
        playerLevel += 1 // Level up
```

```
        playerXP = 0 // Reset XP

        println("Level Up! You are now level $playerLevel")

    }

}
```

This code tracks the player's experience and levels up once they hit a certain XP threshold.

4.2 Understanding Sprites, Animation, and Physics

In game development, creating engaging visuals and smooth interactions is key to drawing players into your game. This is where **sprites**, **animations**, and **physics** come into play. These elements help bring your characters, objects, and world to life. Whether you're building a fast-paced action game or a calm puzzle game, mastering these concepts will help you create dynamic and immersive gameplay.

In this chapter, we'll dive into what sprites are, how animations work, and how physics can make your game world feel real.

What Are Sprites?

A **sprite** is a 2D image or graphic that is used to represent characters, objects, or even parts of a game world. Sprites are typically used for all visible elements in 2D games—like your player character, enemies, obstacles, and other interactive objects.

Sprites are generally drawn onto a **canvas** in a game, and they can be moved around, resized, or even rotated based on the game's logic. Think of sprites as the "actors" in your game's visual story, while the background and environment elements might be static images or tiled textures.

Basic Example: Player Sprite

Let's start by adding a simple sprite to represent a player character in a 2D game.

First, let's load the image of the sprite. For this example, we'll use a `Bitmap` for a simple 2D sprite.

Kotlin

```
// Load the sprite image
val playerBitmap = BitmapFactory.decodeResource(
resources,
R.drawable.player_sprite)
```

```
var playerX = 100f    // X position of player

var playerY = 200f    // Y position of player


// Draw the sprite at the player's position
fun drawPlayer(canvas: Canvas) {

canvas.drawBitmap(playerBitmap, playerX, playerY, null)

}
```

In this code, `playerBitmap` holds the image of the player sprite, and the `drawPlayer` function uses the `Canvas` to display the sprite at the coordinates defined by `playerX` and `playerY`.

Understanding Animation in Games

In games, animation is what makes static images (like sprites) move and change over time. Instead of showing just one image of a character or object, animation involves showing a series of images in quick succession to simulate movement. For example, a walking character might have a sprite that alternates between different frames, each showing a different step in the walk cycle.

Basic Animation Example: Walking Animation

Let's say your player character has multiple frames of animation for walking. We'll use a simple animation sequence where the player's sprite changes every few frames to simulate walking.

1. **Define the frames**: Let's assume we have 4 frames for the walking animation. These frames will be stored in an array.

Kotlin

```
val playerWalkingFrames = arrayOf(

BitmapFactory.decodeResource(
resources,
R.drawable.walk_frame1),

BitmapFactory.decodeResource(
resources,
R.drawable.walk_frame2),
```

```kotlin
BitmapFactory.decodeResource(
resources,
R.drawable.walk_frame3),

BitmapFactory.decodeResource(
resources,
R.drawable.walk_frame4)
)

var currentFrameIndex = 0   // Start with the first frame

var lastUpdateTime = System.currentTimeMillis()
// Track time for frame change
```

2. **Animation Logic**: Now, let's create an animation loop that switches between these frames every 100 milliseconds.

Kotlin

```
fun updateAnimation() {
    val currentTime = System.currentTimeMillis()

    // Change the frame every 100 milliseconds
    if (currentTime - lastUpdateTime > 100) {
        currentFrameIndex = (currentFrameIndex + 1) % playerWalkingFrames.size
```

```
        lastUpdateTime       =
currentTime

    }

}
```

3. **Draw the Animated Sprite**: Finally, we'll draw the current frame to the screen, based on the index of the current animation frame.

Kotlin

```
fun drawPlayerWalking(canvas:
Canvas) {


canvas.drawBitmap(playerWalki
ngFrames[currentFrameIndex],
playerX, playerY, null)
```

}

In this example, `currentFrameIndex` keeps track of which frame of the animation should be shown. We update the frame every 100 milliseconds to create the animation effect. The `drawPlayerWalking` function displays the current frame of the animation at the player's position.

Introduction to Game Physics

Game physics are the rules that govern how objects move and interact in your game world. While **sprites** and **animations** help make the world look interesting, **physics** ensure that the world feels real and consistent. Physics make interactions such as gravity, jumping, bouncing, and collisions behave in a way that is expected by the player.

There are many types of physics to consider in game development. For now, we'll focus on **basic physics** such as gravity and object collision detection.

Basic Physics: Gravity and Jumping

In most games, gravity pulls objects downward. To simulate gravity, we need to update the position of the player in every frame by applying a gravity force that increases over time.

Let's start with simple gravity and jumping mechanics:

Kotlin

```kotlin
var playerVelocityY = 0f   // Vertical velocity of the player (how fast the player is moving up/down)

val gravity = 1f   // Gravity strength

val jumpStrength = -20f   // Strength of the jump


fun updatePlayerPhysics() {

    // Apply gravity to the player's vertical velocity
    playerVelocityY += gravity



    // Update the player's Y position
```

```
    playerY                += playerVelocityY


    // Simulate jumping
    if (isJumping()) {
        playerVelocityY = jumpStrength // Apply jump force
    }


    // Prevent the player from falling below ground
    if (playerY > groundLevel) {
        playerY = groundLevel // Keep the player on the ground
```

```
                playerVelocityY = 0f
// Stop downward movement

        }

}
```

In this code:

- We update the player's vertical velocity (`playerVelocityY`) by adding gravity each frame.
- If the player presses the jump button, we apply a jump strength to make the player move upward.
- The player's Y position is updated based on the velocity, and we prevent the player from falling through the ground by checking if they've gone below a certain `groundLevel`.

Collision Detection

Collision detection is another essential part of physics in game development. It involves checking whether two objects are touching or overlapping in the game world. For example, you might want to check if the player is standing on a platform or if the player collides with an enemy.

Let's assume we have a simple rectangular player and platform. To detect a collision, we check if the player's bounding box (a rectangle surrounding the player) intersects with the platform's bounding box.

Kotlin

```
// Define player and platform bounding boxes
```

```kotlin
val playerRect = RectF(playerX, playerY, playerX + playerBitmap.width, playerY + playerBitmap.height)

val platformRect = RectF(platformX, platformY, platformX + platformWidth, platformY + platformHeight)


// Check for collision
fun checkCollision() {
    if (RectF.intersects(playerRect, platformRect)) {
        println("Collision detected!")
```

```
        // Handle collision
(e.g.,    stop    downward
movement, make player stand
on the platform)
    }
}
```

In this code, the `RectF` objects define rectangular bounding boxes for the player and platform. The `RectF.intersects` method checks if the two rectangles overlap. If they do, we can handle the collision—such as stopping the player's downward movement when they land on a platform.

4.3 Planning Your First Game

Now that we've covered the foundational concepts of game mechanics, sprites, animation, and physics, it's time to take a step back and think about how to plan and structure your first game. While it's tempting to jump straight into coding, taking the time to plan will save you countless hours of frustration and lead to a more polished final product. Whether you're building a simple puzzle game or a more complex action game, planning helps organize your thoughts and establish clear objectives.

In this chapter, we'll go through the essential steps for planning a game—from defining the game's core idea to outlining the design, features, and level progression. You'll even get the chance to storyboard your game idea, a crucial first step in visualizing and organizing your project.

Step 1: Define Your Game Concept

The first and most important step is defining what your game is about. What kind of game do you want to create? Do you want a platformer, a puzzle game, an RPG, or something entirely different? The genre and style of your game will guide everything from gameplay mechanics to visual design and sound.

Key questions to ask:

- What is the core gameplay? (For example, jumping and dodging in a platformer or solving puzzles in a puzzle game)
- What's the goal of the game? (Is it to collect items, defeat enemies, solve puzzles, or complete a series of challenges?)

- Who is your target audience? (Casual gamers, children, hardcore gamers, etc.)
- What's the theme of the game? (For example, space exploration, medieval fantasy, or urban survival)

Let's say you decide to make a simple **2D platformer** where the player must avoid obstacles and collect coins to progress through levels. The goal is to jump over pits and dodge enemies while collecting as many coins as possible.

Step 2: Sketch Your Game's Core Mechanics

Once you've defined your concept, you need to break down the core mechanics—the actions that the player can take in the game. This will include player controls, movement, and interactions with the game world. This is where you'll decide on:

- **Player Movement**: Will your character walk, run, jump, or fly? How will the player interact with the environment (e.g., jumping on platforms, climbing ladders)?
- **Game Progression**: What happens as the player advances through levels? Do they unlock new features or face more challenging enemies?
- **Game Features**: What are the core features of the game? These could be things like power-ups, score tracking, enemies, or environmental hazards.

For our **platformer example**, the core mechanics might look like this:

- **Player Movement**: The player can move left and right using arrow keys or on-screen buttons. The player can jump using a button.
- **Game Objective**: Collect as many coins as possible while avoiding enemies.

- **Challenges**: Obstacles like pits and enemies that move around the screen.

Step 3: Design Your Game's Story and Theme

Even if your game is simple, adding a story and theme can help make the gameplay more engaging. A compelling story helps the player feel connected to the game world and gives them a reason to keep playing.

For our **platformer game**, we could give the player a mission to retrieve a stolen treasure from an evil villain. The player's goal is to navigate through different environments—like forests, caves, and castles—while collecting treasure and avoiding traps.

The theme can tie into your visual design and setting. For instance, if your game is set in a medieval fantasy world, you might choose to use castles, knights, and mythical creatures as your game's visuals and characters.

Step 4: Storyboard Your Game

Storyboarding is a technique used to plan and visualize the flow of the game. It's essentially a sequence of sketches or diagrams that show how the game progresses, from the starting screen to the end. Think of it as a blueprint of your game's visual and gameplay flow.

You don't need to be an artist to create storyboards—simple sketches or flowcharts will do. Storyboarding helps you plan out scenes, level progression, and how players will interact with the game.

For example, here's how you might storyboard your platformer:

1. **Title Screen**: The player sees a title screen with options to start the game or view settings.
2. **Level 1**: The player starts the game and immediately faces obstacles like pits and enemies.
3. **Coin Collection**: As the player progresses, they collect coins for points.
4. **Boss Battle**: The player faces an enemy boss at the end of the level and must defeat it to proceed to the next level.
5. **Level 2**: The player moves to a new environment with new challenges and enemies.
6. **End Screen**: When the player completes the game or loses, they see an end screen with their final score and an option to restart.

You can sketch this out on paper or use digital tools like Figma, Adobe XD, or even PowerPoint to create a flowchart.

Step 5: Choose Your Tools and Resources

At this point, you'll need to decide what tools and resources you'll need to bring your game to life. This includes:

- **Game Engine**: We're using **Android Studio** with **Kotlin** for this book, but other tools like Unity or Godot could be used for larger projects.
- **Graphics**: You can create your own graphics using tools like Photoshop, Illustrator, or free tools like GIMP.

Alternatively, you can find free assets online (just make sure they're licensed for commercial use if necessary).

- **Sound**: Sound effects and background music are important for creating an immersive experience. You can find royalty-free sound effects online or create your own.
- **Other Assets**: Don't forget about other game assets such as backgrounds, platforms, and item icons.

Make sure all assets are organized into appropriate folders in your project, such as:

- **drawable**: For images and sprites
- **raw**: For sounds and music
- **values**: For strings, colors, and other resources

Step 6: Break Down the Game Into Features and Milestones

To avoid feeling overwhelmed, break down your game into smaller, manageable features. Here's a way to think about it:

1. **Core Mechanics**: Implement player movement, jumping, and collision detection.
2. **Game Logic**: Implement the basic game loop, scoring, and win/lose conditions.
3. **Levels and Progression**: Design different levels with increasing difficulty.
4. **Polish**: Add sound effects, animations, and finalize game design.

By breaking your game into smaller pieces, you can work on one part at a time, gradually building up to the finished game. This way, you'll avoid feeling stuck and can easily track your progress.

Step 7: Start Prototyping

At this stage, you should start **prototyping** your game. A prototype is a rough version of your game that you can use to test the core mechanics. Don't worry about perfection—just get the basic functionality working first.

For our platformer example, start by:

- Creating a simple player character that can move left and right.
- Implementing basic collision detection with platforms and obstacles.
- Adding simple enemies or hazards to test the game's challenge.

Once your prototype works, you can start refining it by adding features like animations, sounds, and more levels.

Project: Storyboard a Simple Game Idea (Paper-Based Exercise)

In the last chapter, we explored the importance of planning your game, discussing elements like game mechanics, visuals, and the progression of gameplay. Now, let's dive into one of the most fun and creative parts of game development—storyboarding your game idea. Storyboarding is a way to visually map out your game's flow, levels, and interactions. It doesn't require any fancy software—just pen, paper, and a bit of imagination.

In this project, we will storyboard a simple game idea, mapping out everything from the start screen to the final level. You'll also define the gameplay mechanics, user interface (UI), and level progression. This exercise will help you visualize your game and keep you focused on your goals as you move forward in the development process.

Why Storyboard?

Storyboarding is a technique used in game design to plan the flow of a game. It's an essential step in the development process that gives you a clear idea of how the player will interact with the game, how the game will progress, and how the visuals and mechanics will come together.

Here are a few reasons why storyboarding is crucial for game development:

- **Clear Game Flow**: Storyboarding helps define the sequence of events in your game, making sure that everything flows logically.
- **Level Design**: It helps visualize the levels and interactions within each level, from beginning to end.

- **Efficiency**: Storyboarding gives you a roadmap, helping to reduce confusion and development errors.
- **Communication**: If you're working with a team, storyboards are a great way to communicate your ideas with designers, artists, and programmers.

Now, let's get started on creating your storyboard.

Step 1: Game Concept Overview

Before you begin sketching, let's take a moment to briefly define the concept of the game you want to create. It doesn't have to be complex, but it's important to have a clear vision of what your game will be.

For this exercise, let's use a simple **2D Platformer** idea as an example. Here's a basic overview of the game:

- **Game Title**: "Jump Quest"
- **Genre**: 2D Platformer
- **Objective**: The player needs to jump across platforms, avoid enemies, and collect coins to reach the end of each level.
- **Setting**: A bright, colorful fantasy world with forests, caves, and castles.
- **Player Character**: A small adventurer with the ability to jump and run.
- **Goal**: Collect all the coins in each level and reach the finish line to advance to the next level.

Step 2: Sketch the Main Screens

Start by drawing the main screens that the player will encounter in your game. This is where you'll define the layout, UI elements, and general look of the game.

1. Title Screen

The title screen is the first thing the player will see. It should be simple, yet engaging. Include the following elements in your sketch:

- **Game Title**: The name of your game (e.g., "Jump Quest").
- **Play Button**: A button that will start the game.
- **Settings Button**: A button for the player to access settings (such as sound options).
- **High Scores**: A way to view the player's highest scores.
- **Background**: You can sketch a simple background to set the mood of the game (perhaps a bright, fantasy-themed landscape).

Example Sketch:

less

```
+-----------------------------
+
```

```
|            Jump Quest
|

|
|

|         [Play]
[Settings]      |

|
|

|        High Scores: [1000]
|

|
|

|        (Background image)
|
+-----------------------------+
```

2. Game UI Screen

Now, sketch what the player will see during the game. This includes:

- **Player Character**: Where the player's character will appear (e.g., in the bottom-left corner).
- **Score**: A UI element displaying the current score (e.g., the number of coins collected).
- **Lives**: If your game has a life system, draw a UI element for displaying the player's remaining lives.
- **Game World**: The background and platforms where the player will interact.
- **Buttons**: Controls for the player (e.g., jump, run).

Example Sketch:

less

```
+-------------------------- - -
+
```

```
|  Score: 50          Lives: 3
|
|
|
|
|
|           [ Player Character ]
|
|
|
|  (Platform 1)      (Platform 2)           |
|        [ Coin ]          [ Coin ]         |
|
|
```

```
|              (Background Image)
|
+-----------------------------
+
```

Step 3: Define the Levels

Next, think about how your game will progress through levels. In this section of the storyboard, sketch the layout of the first few levels and define their main challenges.

For each level, ask yourself the following questions:

- What is the layout of the level? How will platforms be arranged?
- Are there any obstacles or enemies in the level?
- Where are the coins or other collectibles placed?

- How does the player progress to the next level (e.g., reaching a flag, collecting all coins, etc.)?

Example Level 1:

- **Layout**: The level starts with a flat ground, a few platforms to jump on, and a couple of coins scattered across the level.
- **Challenges**: Some platforms are moving, requiring the player to time their jumps carefully. A small enemy patrols one of the platforms.
- **Goal**: Collect all the coins and reach the flag at the end of the level.

Example Level 2:

- **Layout**: The player starts on a higher platform with a gap to cross. The platforms are smaller, and some are

located in the air, requiring the player to jump at the right moment.
- **Challenges**: A larger enemy boss appears at the end of the level.
- **Goal**: Defeat the boss and proceed to the next stage.

Step 4: Draw the Flowchart

A flowchart is a simple, visual representation of the game's progression. It helps you outline how the player moves from one screen or level to the next. Create a simple flowchart to represent the sequence of events in your game. This could include the following stages:

1. **Start Screen**: The player clicks the Play button.
2. **Level 1**: The player progresses through the level, collecting coins and avoiding enemies.

3. **Victory Screen**: After completing Level 1, the player is shown a victory screen with their score and options to continue to the next level or return to the main menu.
4. **Level 2**: If the player chooses to continue, they move to Level 2.
5. **End Screen**: If the player loses all their lives, they are shown a game-over screen with options to restart or quit.

Example Flowchart:

sql

```
+----------------------+
+------------------+
|   Title Screen      |  ---->
|   Level 1          |
```

| (Play / Settings) |
| (Collect Coins) |

+--------------------+
+----------------+

|

+------------------+

                            |

Level 1 Complete |

+------------------+

|

+----------------+

```
Level 2        |
                              |
(New Challenges) |
                              |
+------------------+

|

+------------------+
                              |
Game Over      |

+------------------+
```

Step 5: Final Thoughts

Storyboarding is an excellent way to bring your game idea to life before you start coding. It forces you to think critically about the gameplay, user experience, and design elements, and ensures that your game is fun, engaging, and playable from the very beginning.

You don't need to be a professional artist to create a great storyboard—simple sketches or flowcharts will work just fine. The goal is to create a blueprint for your game that you can refer to as you develop and refine it.

In the next chapter, we'll begin turning these plans into actual game code, bringing your storyboard to life. But for now, take your time with this exercise, and really think about how the game will unfold from start to finish. The better you plan, the smoother your development process will be!

Your Assignment:

- Create storyboards for your game, including the title screen, UI, gameplay, and level design.
- Draw a flowchart to represent how your game will progress from start to finish.
- Keep it simple, but make sure you capture the key features and mechanics.

In this chapter, we've covered the key elements of game design, from game mechanics to sprites, animations, and physics. You learned how to storyboard your first game idea, which is an essential skill for creating engaging, well-thought-out games. As you continue developing your game, keep these foundational concepts in mind—they'll guide you as you bring your ideas to life.

Chapter 5: Creating Your First 2D Game

In this chapter, we'll begin creating our first 2D game step-by-step. Starting with the essential building blocks, you'll learn how to set up a game loop, draw sprites, handle collisions, and make the game interactive. By the end of this chapter, you'll have a working game—a simple "Catch the Ball" game.

5.1 Setting Up a Game Loop

At the heart of any game lies the **game loop**. It's the mechanism that ensures the game runs smoothly, allowing updates to the game state and rendering visuals consistently. This section will guide you through building a game loop step-by-step, explaining its components and how it powers a game.

What is a Game Loop?

The game loop is a repeating sequence of operations that manage the game's progress and visuals. It consists of three main parts:

1. **Initialize**: Set up the game (e.g., load resources, initialize variables).
2. **Update**: Change the state of the game (e.g., move objects, process input).
3. **Render**: Draw the updated game state to the screen.

The loop typically runs continuously until the game is exited or paused. Its constant repetition creates the perception of motion and interactivity.

Why is a Game Loop Important?

In a game, actions like animations, movement, and collisions need to happen over time rather than instantaneously. The game loop provides the framework for these operations, ensuring the game reacts and renders smoothly.

Step-by-Step: Building a Game Loop in Kotlin

1. **Create a New Android Project**:
    - Open Android Studio.
    - Create a new project using an **Empty Activity**.
    - Name your project (e.g., "GameLoopExample").
    - Set the minimum SDK to at least **API Level 21 (Lollipop)** for broader compatibility.
2. **Set Up a Custom View**: Android doesn't provide a direct game loop API,

but we can build one using a `SurfaceView` and a background thread. The `SurfaceView` allows us to control drawing to the screen efficiently.

Code Implementation

Step 1: Create a GameView Class

Create a new class `GameView` that extends `SurfaceView` and implements `Runnable`.

Kotlin

```
package com.example.gameloopexample

import android.content.Context
```

```
import android.graphics.Canvas
import android.graphics.Color
import android.graphics.Paint
import android.util.AttributeSet
import android.view.SurfaceHolder
import android.view.SurfaceView


class GameView(context: Context) : SurfaceView(context), Runnable {
```

```
    private var isPlaying = 
false // Flag to control the 
game loop

    private val thread = 
Thread(this) // Thread to run 
the game loop

    private val paint = 
Paint() // Paint object for 
drawing

    private lateinit var 
canvas: Canvas // Canvas to 
draw on


    init {

        // Set the 
SurfaceView's holder callback
```

```kotlin
holder.addCallback(object :
SurfaceHolder.Callback {

    override fun surfaceCreated(holder:
SurfaceHolder) {

        // Start the game loop when the surface is created

        start()
    }


    override fun surfaceChanged(

        holder: SurfaceHolder,

        format: Int,
```

```kotlin
            width: Int,
            height: Int
        ) {}

        override fun surfaceDestroyed(holder: SurfaceHolder) {
            // Stop the game loop when the surface is destroyed
            stop()
        }
    })
}
```

```kotlin
override fun run() {
    while (isPlaying) {
        update()    // Update the game state
        draw()      // Render the updated state
        control()   // Control the frame rate
    }
}

private fun update() {
    // Update game logic (e.g., move objects, check collisions)
}
```

```kotlin
    private fun draw() {
        if (holder.surface.isValid) {
            canvas = holder.lockCanvas()

            canvas.drawColor(Color.BLACK) // Clear the screen with black color
            paint.color = Color.WHITE
            paint.textSize = 50f

            // Example: Draw text and a circle
```

```
canvas.drawText("Game    Loop Running", 50f, 100f, paint)

canvas.drawCircle(width / 2f, height / 2f, 50f, paint)



holder.unlockCanvasAndPost(canvas) // Post the updated frame

        }
    }


    private fun control() {
        try {
```

```kotlin
            // Sleep to control the frame rate (60 FPS = ~16ms per frame)
            Thread.sleep(16)
        } catch (e: InterruptedException) {
            e.printStackTrace()
        }
    }

    fun start() {
        isPlaying = true
        thread.start()
    }
```

```kotlin
fun stop() {
    isPlaying = false
    try {
        thread.join()  // Wait for the thread to finish
    } catch (e: InterruptedException) {
        e.printStackTrace()
    }
}
```

Step 2: Update MainActivity

Set the `GameView` as the content view in the `MainActivity`.

Kotlin

```
package com.example.gameloopexample

import android.os.Bundle
import androidx.appcompat.app.AppCompatActivity

class MainActivity : AppCompatActivity() {
```

```kotlin
    private lateinit var gameView: GameView


    override fun onCreate(savedInstanceState: Bundle?) {

        super.onCreate(savedInstanceState)

        // Initialize GameView and set it as the content view
        gameView = GameView(this)

        setContentView(gameView)
```

```kotlin
    }

    override fun onPause() {
        super.onPause()
        // Stop the game loop when the activity is paused
        gameView.stop()
    }

    override fun onResume() {
        super.onResume()
        // Restart the game loop when the activity is resumed
        gameView.start()
```

        }
    }

Testing Your Game Loop

1. Run the app on an emulator or a real device.
2. You should see a black screen with a white circle and the text "Game Loop Running."

Enhancements to Consider

- **Frame Rate Display**: Measure and display the current frames per second (FPS).

- **Dynamic Content**: Add moving objects or animations to visualize the loop's functionality.

5.2 Drawing Sprites and Handling Collisions

Drawing sprites and detecting collisions are fundamental to building any interactive game. Sprites represent visual objects in the game, such as characters, obstacles, or collectibles, while collision handling ensures meaningful interactions, like a character collecting a coin or hitting an obstacle.

This section walks you through how to create and manipulate sprites, and how to implement basic collision detection, all in **Kotlin** using Android's `Canvas` and `Rect` classes.

What is a Sprite?

A **sprite** is a 2D image or object that can be displayed and manipulated on the screen. Sprites can represent characters, backgrounds, items, or any visual component in your game.

Key Concepts

1. **Bitmap**: Represents the graphical content of a sprite.
2. **Canvas**: Used to draw the sprites on the screen.
3. **Collision Detection**: Involves checking if two objects overlap (e.g., when a player touches an enemy or a collectible).

Setting Up Sprites

To work with sprites, we'll use `Bitmap` objects. Let's start by creating a sprite and moving it across the screen.

Step-by-Step Implementation

Step 1: Prepare a Sprite Image

- Add a sprite image to your project.
    - Place the image in the `res/drawable` folder (e.g., `res/drawable/sprite.png`).

Step 2: Create the GameView

Enhance the `GameView` class from the previous section to include sprite drawing and movement.

Kotlin

```
package com.example.spriteexample

import android.content.Context

import android.graphics.*

import android.view.SurfaceHolder

import android.view.SurfaceView


class GameView(context: Context) : SurfaceView(context), Runnable {
```

```kotlin
    private var isPlaying = false // Controls the game loop
    private val thread = Thread(this) // Game loop thread
    private lateinit var canvas: Canvas // Canvas for drawing
    private val paint = Paint() // Paint object for drawing
    private val surfaceHolder: SurfaceHolder = holder
```

```
private lateinit var spriteBitmap: Bitmap // Sprite image

private var spriteX = 100f // X position of the sprite

private var spriteY = 100f // Y position of the sprite

private var spriteSpeedX = 10f // Horizontal speed

private var spriteSpeedY = 10f // Vertical speed


init {
    // Load the sprite image from resources
```

```kotlin
    spriteBitmap = BitmapFactory.decodeResource(resources, R.drawable.sprite)
    }


    override fun run() {
        while (isPlaying) {
            update()     // Update sprite position
            draw()       // Draw updated state
            control()    // Control frame rate
        }
    }
```

```
private fun update() {
    // Update sprite position
    spriteX += spriteSpeedX
    spriteY += spriteSpeedY


    // Reverse direction if the sprite hits screen edges
    if (spriteX < 0 || spriteX + spriteBitmap.width > width) {
        spriteSpeedX = -spriteSpeedX
    }
```

```
        if (spriteY < 0 ||
spriteY + spriteBitmap.height
> height) {

            spriteSpeedY = -
spriteSpeedY

        }

    }


    private fun draw() {

        if
(surfaceHolder.surface.isVali
d) {

            canvas           =
surfaceHolder.lockCanvas()


canvas.drawColor(Color.BLACK)
// Clear the screen
```

```
            // Draw the sprite
canvas.drawBitmap(spriteBitmap, spriteX, spriteY, paint)



surfaceHolder.unlockCanvasAndPost(canvas) // Post the updated frame
        }
    }


    private fun control() {
        try {
```

```kotlin
            Thread.sleep(16) // ~60 FPS
        } catch (e: InterruptedException) {
            e.printStackTrace()
        }
    }

    fun start() {
        isPlaying = true
        thread.start()
    }

    fun stop() {
```

```
            isPlaying = false

            try {

                thread.join()

            } catch (e: InterruptedException) {

                e.printStackTrace()

            }

        }

    }
```

Step 3: Update the MainActivity

Update your `MainActivity` to use the enhanced `GameView`.

Kotlin

```kotlin
package com.example.spriteexample

import android.os.Bundle
import androidx.appcompat.app.AppCompatActivity

class MainActivity : AppCompatActivity() {

    private lateinit var gameView: GameView
```

```kotlin
override fun onCreate(savedInstanceState: Bundle?) {

super.onCreate(savedInstanceState)

    gameView = GameView(this)

setContentView(gameView)
    }


    override fun onPause() {
        super.onPause()
        gameView.stop()
```

```
    }


    override fun onResume() {
        super.onResume()
        gameView.start()
    }
}
```

Handling Collisions

Now that we have a moving sprite, let's add collision detection. This example checks whether the sprite collides with a fixed object on the screen.

Adding Collision Detection

Step 1: Define a Target Object

Add a target object represented by a rectangle.

Kotlin

```
private val targetRect = Rect(300, 300, 400, 400) // Target area
```

Step 2: Check for Collisions

Add a function to check if the sprite overlaps with the target rectangle.

Kotlin

```
private fun isColliding(): Boolean {
```

```kotlin
    val spriteRect = Rect(
        spriteX.toInt(),
        spriteY.toInt(),
        (spriteX + spriteBitmap.width).toInt(),
        (spriteY + spriteBitmap.height).toInt()
    )
    return Rect.intersects(spriteRect, targetRect)
}
```

Step 3: Update Drawing Logic

Update the draw function to visualize the collision.

Kotlin

```kotlin
private fun draw() {
    if (surfaceHolder.surface.isValid) {
        canvas = surfaceHolder.lockCanvas()

        canvas.drawColor(Color.BLACK) // Clear the screen

        // Draw the target rectangle
        paint.color = if (isColliding()) Color.RED else Color.GREEN
```

```
canvas.drawRect(targetRect, paint)

        // Draw the sprite

canvas.drawBitmap(spriteBitmap, spriteX, spriteY, paint)



surfaceHolder.unlockCanvasAndPost(canvas)
    }
}
```

When the sprite touches the target, the rectangle will change color to red, indicating a collision.

5.3 Adding User Interactivity

User interactivity brings games to life. It allows players to control characters, navigate menus, or interact with the environment. In this chapter, you'll learn how to handle user input in Android games, whether it's via touch, gestures, or sensors.

Overview of User Input in Android

Android provides multiple ways to capture user input for games:

1. **Touch Events**: Detect single or multi-touch gestures like taps, drags, and swipes.
2. **Sensors**: Access accelerometer, gyroscope, or other sensors for motion-based input.
3. **Hardware Input**: Handle key events from physical or virtual keyboards and controllers.

For simplicity, we'll focus on **touch input** in this chapter, as it is the most commonly used interaction mechanism in mobile games.

Setting Up Touch Input

To capture touch events, override the `onTouchEvent` method in your `GameView`. This method receives all touch-related input, such as down, move, and up events.

Step 1: Enhance the `GameView`

We'll add functionality to move a sprite based on touch input.

Code Implementation:

Kotlin

```
package com.example.interactivityexample


import android.content.Context

import android.graphics.*

import android.view.MotionEvent
```

```
import android.view.SurfaceHolder

import android.view.SurfaceView


class GameView(context: Context) : SurfaceView(context), Runnable {

    private var isPlaying = false // Controls the game loop

    private val thread = Thread(this) // Game loop thread

    private lateinit var canvas: Canvas // Canvas for drawing
```

```kotlin
    private val paint = Paint() // Paint object for drawing

    private val surfaceHolder: SurfaceHolder = holder


    private lateinit var spriteBitmap: Bitmap // Sprite image

    private var spriteX = 100f // X position of the sprite

    private var spriteY = 100f // Y position of the sprite

    init {
```

```
        // Load the sprite image from resources
        spriteBitmap = BitmapFactory.decodeResource(resources, R.drawable.sprite)
    }


    override fun run() {
        while (isPlaying) {
            draw()     // Draw updated state
            control()      // Control frame rate
        }
    }
```

```kotlin
private fun draw() {
    if (surfaceHolder.surface.isValid) {
        canvas = surfaceHolder.lockCanvas()

        canvas.drawColor(Color.BLACK) // Clear the screen

        // Draw the sprite
        canvas.drawBitmap(spriteBitmap, spriteX, spriteY, paint)
```

```
        surfaceHolder.unlockCanvasAndPost(canvas)  // Post the updated frame
            }
        }


        private fun control() {
            try {
                Thread.sleep(16)  // ~60 FPS
            } catch (e: InterruptedException) {
                e.printStackTrace()
            }
```

```kotlin
    }


    // Handle touch input
    override fun onTouchEvent(event: MotionEvent): Boolean {
        when (event.action) {

            MotionEvent.ACTION_DOWN -> {
                // Move the sprite to the touch location
                spriteX = event.x - spriteBitmap.width / 2
                spriteY = event.y - spriteBitmap.height / 2
```

```kotlin
            }
        }
        return true // Indicate the event was handled
    }


    fun start() {
        isPlaying = true
        thread.start()
    }


    fun stop() {
        isPlaying = false
        try {
```

```
                thread.join()
        }      catch      (e: InterruptedException) {

e.printStackTrace()
            }
        }
}
```

Explanation:

- The onTouchEvent method captures the touch input.
- The ACTION_DOWN event triggers when the screen is touched.
- The sprite moves to the touch location, centering it around the touch point.

Step 2: Update the MainActivity

Ensure your `MainActivity` uses the enhanced `GameView`.

Kotlin

```
package com.example.interactivityexample

import android.os.Bundle
import androidx.appcompat.app.AppCompatActivity

class MainActivity : AppCompatActivity() {
```

```kotlin
    private    lateinit    var gameView: GameView


    override                fun onCreate(savedInstanceState: Bundle?) {

super.onCreate(savedInstanceState)

        gameView           = GameView(this)

setContentView(gameView)

    }


    override fun onPause() {
```

```
        super.onPause()

        gameView.stop()

    }


    override fun onResume() {

        super.onResume()

        gameView.start()

    }
}
```

Adding Gesture Controls

For more complex input, Android supports gestures like swipes and drags. Let's implement drag functionality.

Step 1: Enhance the onTouchEvent

Modify onTouchEvent to handle dragging.

Kotlin

```kotlin
private var isDragging = false

override fun onTouchEvent(event: MotionEvent): Boolean {
    when (event.action) {
        MotionEvent.ACTION_DOWN -> {
            // Check if the touch is within the sprite's bounds
```

```
            if   (event.x    >= 
spriteX && event.x <= spriteX 
+ spriteBitmap.width && 

               event.y     >= 
spriteY && event.y <= spriteY 
+ spriteBitmap.height 

               ) { 

                  isDragging   = 
true 

               } 

          } 


MotionEvent.ACTION_MOVE -> { 

            if (isDragging) { 

                   //      Update 
sprite position during drag
```

```
                spriteX         =
event.x   -   spriteBitmap.width
/ 2

                spriteY         =
event.y   -   spriteBitmap.height
/ 2

                }

            }

        MotionEvent.ACTION_UP
-> {

                isDragging       =
false // End the drag

            }

        }

    return true

}
```

Explanation:

- The ACTION_DOWN event checks if the touch starts within the sprite's bounds.
- During ACTION_MOVE, the sprite follows the touch position.
- The ACTION_UP event ends the drag.

Adding Multi-Touch

Multi-touch allows players to control multiple elements simultaneously, such as moving two objects or zooming.

Step 1: Detect Multi-Touch Points

Add functionality to track multiple touch points.

Kotlin

```kotlin
override fun onTouchEvent(event: MotionEvent): Boolean {
    for (i in 0 until event.pointerCount) {
        val pointerId = event.getPointerId(i)
        val x = event.getX(i)
        val y = event.getY(i)


        // Handle each touch point individually
        if (pointerId == 0) {
            // Move sprite 1
```

```
            spriteX  =  x -
spriteBitmap.width / 2
            spriteY  =  y -
spriteBitmap.height / 2
        } else if (pointerId
== 1) {
            // Handle another
sprite or action
        }
    }
    return true
}
```

Explanation:

- `pointerCount` tracks how many fingers are touching the screen.

- Each pointer's position (x, y) is retrieved and handled independently.

Project: Build a Simple "Catch the Ball" Game

This hands-on project will guide you through building a simple 2D game called *Catch the Ball*. The game mechanics are straightforward: balls fall from the top of the screen, and the player must move a basket to catch them. It's a fun way to practice handling animations, collisions, and user interactivity in game development.

Project Breakdown

Features:

- Balls randomly spawn and fall toward the bottom of the screen.
- A movable basket controlled by the player catches the balls.
- Score increases when a ball is caught.

Step 1: Setting Up the Game Structure

We'll use the **SurfaceView** class to create a game loop and manage rendering. Start by creating the project and setting up the necessary components.

Create the Project

1. Open Android Studio and create a new project.
2. Choose **Empty Activity** and name it `CatchTheBallGame`.

3. Set the programming language to **Kotlin**.

File Structure:

- `MainActivity.kt`: Entry point for the game.
- `GameView.kt`: Core game logic and rendering.
- `Ball.kt`: Represents the falling ball.
- `Basket.kt`: Represents the player-controlled basket.

Step 2: GameView - Core of the Game

Create a new `GameView` class for the game logic.

Code for `GameView.kt`:

Kotlin

```
package com.example.catchtheballgame

import android.content.Context

import android.graphics.*

import android.view.MotionEvent

import android.view.SurfaceHolder

import android.view.SurfaceView

import Kotlin.random.Random
```

```kotlin
class GameView(context: Context) : SurfaceView(context), Runnable {

    private var isPlaying = true

    private val thread = Thread(this)

    private val surfaceHolder: SurfaceHolder = holder

    private val paint = Paint()


    private val balls = mutableListOf<Ball>() // List of falling balls
```

```kotlin
    private val basket = Basket(context.resources)  // The basket
    private var score = 0 // Player's score


    init {
        // Spawn initial balls
        for (i in 0..4) {
            balls.add(Ball(context.resources))
        }
    }
```

```kotlin
override fun run() {
    while (isPlaying) {
        update()
        draw()
        control()
    }
}


private fun update() {
    // Update all balls
    for (ball in balls) {
        ball.update()
```

```
            // Check for
collision with the basket
            if
(Rect.intersects(ball.getRect
(), basket.getRect())) {
                score++

ball.resetPosition()      //
Respawn the ball

            }


            // Remove ball if
it falls off the screen
            if (ball.y >
height) {

ball.resetPosition()
```

            }
        }
    }

        private fun draw() {
            if (surfaceHolder.surface.isValid) {
                val canvas = surfaceHolder.lockCanvas()

canvas.drawColor(Color.BLACK) // Clear the screen

                // Draw balls

```
            for (ball in balls) {
                ball.draw(canvas, paint)
            }

            // Draw basket
            basket.draw(canvas, paint)

            // Draw score
            paint.color = Color.WHITE
            paint.textSize = 60f
```

```kotlin
            canvas.drawText("Score: $score", 50f, 100f, paint)


            surfaceHolder.unlockCanvasAndPost(canvas)
        }
    }


    private fun control() {
        Thread.sleep(16)    // ~60 FPS
    }
```

```kotlin
    override fun onTouchEvent(event: MotionEvent): Boolean {
        // Move basket with touch
        when (event.action) {
            MotionEvent.ACTION_MOVE -> {
                basket.x = event.x - basket.width / 2
            }
        }
        return true
    }

    fun start() {
```

```
        isPlaying = true

        thread.start()

    }



    fun stop() {

        isPlaying = false

        try {

            thread.join()

        }      catch      (e: InterruptedException) {

e.printStackTrace()

        }

    }

}
```

Step 3: Ball Class

The `Ball` class handles the logic for each falling ball.

Code for `Ball.kt`:

Kotlin

```
package com.example.catchtheballgame

import android.content.res.Resources
```

```kotlin
import android.graphics.Bitmap

import android.graphics.BitmapFactory

import android.graphics.Rect

import Kotlin.random.Random


class Ball(resources: Resources) {

    private var bitmap: Bitmap = BitmapFactory.decodeResource(resources, R.drawable.ball)

    var x: Float = Random.nextInt(100, 700).toFloat()  // Random start X position
```

```kotlin
    var y: Float = -100f // Start above the screen
    private var speed: Float = Random.nextInt(5, 15).toFloat()    // Random falling speed


    fun update() {
        y += speed
    }


    fun resetPosition() {
        x = Random.nextInt(100, 700).toFloat()
        y = -100f
```

```kotlin
        speed = Random.nextInt(5, 15).toFloat()
    }

    fun draw(canvas: Canvas, paint: Paint) {
        canvas.drawBitmap(bitmap, x, y, paint)
    }

    fun getRect(): Rect {
        return Rect(x.toInt(), y.toInt(), (x + bitmap.width).toInt(), (y + bitmap.height).toInt())
```

        }
}

Step 4: Basket Class

The `Basket` class represents the player's control.

Code for `Basket.kt`:

Kotlin

```
package com.example.catchtheballgame

import android.content.res.Resources
```

```
import android.graphics.Bitmap

import android.graphics.BitmapFactory

import android.graphics.Canvas

import android.graphics.Paint

import android.graphics.Rect


class Basket(resources: Resources) {

    private var bitmap: Bitmap = BitmapFactory.decodeResource(resources, R.drawable.basket)

    var x: Float = 400f
```

```kotlin
    var y: Float = 1200f

    val width: Int = bitmap.width

    val height: Int = bitmap.height


    fun draw(canvas: Canvas, paint: Paint) {

canvas.drawBitmap(bitmap, x, y, paint)

    }


    fun getRect(): Rect {
        return Rect(x.toInt(), y.toInt(), (x
```

```
+   width).toInt(),    (y   +
height).toInt())

    }
}
```

Step 5: Update MainActivity

Update the `MainActivity` to use the `GameView`.

Code for `MainActivity.kt`:

Kotlin

```
package
com.example.catchtheballgame
```

```kotlin
import android.os.Bundle
import androidx.appcompat.app.AppCompatActivity

class MainActivity : AppCompatActivity() {

    private lateinit var gameView: GameView

    override fun onCreate(savedInstanceState: Bundle?) {

        super.onCreate(savedInstanceState)
```

```kotlin
        gameView =
GameView(this)

setContentView(gameView)
    }


    override fun onPause() {
        super.onPause()
        gameView.stop()
    }


    override fun onResume() {
        super.onResume()
        gameView.start()
    }
```

}

Step 6: Add Assets

Place images for the **ball** (`ball.png`) and **basket** (`basket.png`) in the `res/drawable` folder.

Congratulations! You've built a simple yet functional "Catch the Ball" game. This project introduced you to game loops, sprite handling, collision detection, and user interactivity. These are foundational skills you'll use as you tackle more complex games in the future.

Chapter 6: Working with Graphics and Animations

In game development, visuals play a significant role in enhancing the player's experience. This chapter explores how to use Android's graphics tools to draw, customize, and animate game elements. You'll learn to work with the **Canvas** API, handle bitmap and vector assets, and create dynamic animations that bring your game to life.

6.1 Customizing Canvas and Drawing API

Drawing graphics directly on the screen is a fundamental part of game development. In Android, the **Canvas** and **Paint** classes are the primary tools for rendering custom visuals. This section will guide you through the basics of using the Canvas API to draw shapes, text, and images while customizing styles with the Paint class.

Understanding the Canvas API

The Canvas API acts as a virtual drawing surface where you can create graphics programmatically. You can think of it as your blank canvas, and everything you draw—shapes, text, or images—appears on this canvas.

Core Canvas Methods

Here are some of the most commonly used methods in the Canvas API:

- `drawRect(Rect, Paint)` or `drawRect(left, top, right, bottom, Paint)`: Draws a rectangle.

- `drawCircle(float cx, float cy, float radius, Paint)`: Draws a circle.
- `drawLine(float startX, float startY, float stopX, float stopY, Paint)`: Draws a line.
- `drawText(String text, float x, float y, Paint)`: Draws text.
- `drawBitmap(Bitmap bitmap, float left, float top, Paint)`: Draws a bitmap image.

Using Paint for Styling

The **Paint** class works alongside Canvas to define how the shapes, text, or images appear. It allows you to set:

- **Colors**:
  `paint.setColor(Color.RED)`
- **Text Size**:
  `paint.setTextSize(40f)`
- **Line Thickness**:
  `paint.setStrokeWidth(5f)`
- **Anti-aliasing**:
  `paint.setAntiAlias(true)`
  (for smoother edges)

Example: Drawing Shapes on Canvas

Let's create a simple example to draw a rectangle, a circle, and a line on the screen.

Step 1: Setting up a Custom View

Create a custom `View` class where you'll override the `onDraw()` method.

Kotlin

```
class CustomDrawingView(context: Context) : View(context) {

    private val paint = Paint().apply {
        isAntiAlias = true // Smooth edges
        style = Paint.Style.FILL // Default: FILL; others: STROKE, FILL_AND_STROKE
    }
```

```kotlin
override fun onDraw(canvas: Canvas) {
    super.onDraw(canvas)

    // Draw a red rectangle
    paint.color = Color.RED
    canvas.drawRect(100f, 100f, 400f, 400f, paint)

    // Draw a blue circle
    paint.color = Color.BLUE
    canvas.drawCircle(250f, 600f, 100f, paint)
```

```
// Draw a green line
paint.color = Color.GREEN
paint.strokeWidth = 10f
canvas.drawLine(100f, 800f, 400f, 1000f, paint)


// Draw some text
paint.color = Color.BLACK
paint.textSize = 50f

canvas.drawText("Hello, Canvas!", 100f, 1100f, paint)
```

}
}

Step 2: Adding the Custom View to Your Activity

In your activity, replace the default layout with the custom view:

Kotlin

```
class MainActivity : AppCompatActivity() {
    override fun onCreate(savedInstanceState: Bundle?) {
```

```kotlin
super.onCreate(savedInstanceState)

    // Set CustomDrawingView as the content view
    val drawingView = CustomDrawingView(this)
    setContentView(drawingView)
    }
}
```

When you run the app, you'll see a red rectangle, a blue circle, a green line, and some black text on the screen.

Working with Text on Canvas

To display text, use the `drawText()` method. You can customize the appearance of the text using the `Paint` class.

Code Example: Drawing Text

Kotlin

```
paint.color = Color.MAGENTA

paint.textSize = 60f

canvas.drawText("Welcome to Game Dev!", 50f, 1200f, paint)
```

Useful Properties:

- **textSize**: Sets the font size.
- **textAlign**: Aligns text (`Paint.Align.LEFT`, `CENTER`, `RIGHT`).
- **typeface**: Sets the font style using `Typeface`.

Optimizing for Performance

To avoid redrawing everything repeatedly:

1. Use **double buffering** by caching your drawings in a `Bitmap`.
2. Call `invalidate()` selectively to redraw only parts of the screen that need updates.

Interactive Shapes: Adding Motion

A game isn't static! Let's add motion to a shape. Update the shape's position dynamically using a handler.

Code Example: Moving a Circle

Kotlin

```kotlin
class MovingCircleView(context: Context) : View(context) {

    private val paint = Paint().apply { color = Color.CYAN }

    private var x = 100f
```

```kotlin
private var y = 100f
private var speedX = 10f
private var speedY = 15f


override fun onDraw(canvas: Canvas) {
    super.onDraw(canvas)


    // Draw the circle
    canvas.drawCircle(x, y, 50f, paint)


    // Update position
    x += speedX
    y += speedY
```

```
        // Reverse direction if the circle hits the edges
        if (x <= 50 || x >= width - 50) speedX = -speedX
        if (y <= 50 || y >= height - 50) speedY = -speedY


        // Redraw the view
        invalidate()
    }
}
```

Project: Draw a Game Background

Let's implement a basic game background using the Canvas API. We'll draw a gradient sky, a sun, and a grassy ground.

Step 1: Define the Custom View

Kotlin

```
class GameBackgroundView(context: Context) : View(context) {

    private val paint = Paint()
```

```kotlin
override fun onDraw(canvas: Canvas) {
    super.onDraw(canvas)

    // Draw gradient sky
    val gradient = LinearGradient(
        0f, 0f, 0f, height.toFloat(),
        Color.CYAN, Color.BLUE,
        Shader.TileMode.CLAMP
    )
    paint.shader = gradient
```

```
        canvas.drawRect(0f,
0f,         width.toFloat(),
height.toFloat(), paint)


        // Draw the sun

        paint.shader = null

        paint.color          =
Color.YELLOW


canvas.drawCircle(width / 2f,
height / 4f, 100f, paint)


        // Draw the ground

        paint.color          =
Color.GREEN

        canvas.drawRect(0f,
height         -         300f,
```

```
width.toFloat(),
height.toFloat(), paint)
    }
}
```

Step 2: Add the View to an Activity

Kotlin

```
override                    fun
onCreate(savedInstanceState:
Bundle?) {

super.onCreate(savedInstanceS
tate)

setContentView(GameBackground
View(this))
```

}

6.2 Using Bitmap and Vector Assets in Your Games

Images are essential in game design, whether they are characters, backgrounds, or objects that make your game visually appealing. In Android development, **Bitmap** and **Vector assets** are two primary types of image formats you can use.

This chapter will explore:

1. **Bitmap assets**: How to work with raster images like PNGs and JPGs.
2. **Vector assets**: The advantages of using scalable graphics in your games.
3. How to use these assets effectively within your game.

Understanding Bitmap Assets

Bitmaps are raster images made of pixels. They are perfect for rich, detailed graphics but can lose quality when scaled up or down. Common formats include PNG, JPG, and WEBP.

Loading Bitmaps in Android

To load a bitmap in your game, Android provides the `BitmapFactory` class.

Example: Loading a Bitmap

First, add an image to your `res/drawable` folder (e.g., `ball.png`).

Kotlin

```
val bitmap =
BitmapFactory.decodeResource(
resources, R.drawable.ball)
```

Drawing a Bitmap on Canvas

You can use the `Canvas.drawBitmap()` method to display the bitmap.

Kotlin

```
class BitmapGameView(context:
Context) : View(context) {

    private val ball: Bitmap =
BitmapFactory.decodeResource(
resources, R.drawable.ball)
```

```kotlin
    override fun onDraw(canvas: Canvas) {
        super.onDraw(canvas)

        // Draw the bitmap at (100, 100)
        canvas.drawBitmap(ball, 100f, 100f, null)
    }
}
```

Optimizing Bitmaps

Since large bitmaps can consume memory, optimizing them is critical in game development.

Scaling Bitmaps

Use `Bitmap.createScaledBitmap()` to resize an image.

Kotlin

```
val scaledBall = Bitmap.createScaledBitmap(ball, 200, 200, true)
```

Reducing Bitmap Size

If the bitmap is too large for your device memory:

- Use a lower resolution image.
- Compress the image with the `WEBP` format.

Recycling Bitmaps

Always release unused bitmaps to free up memory.

Kotlin

```
ball.recycle()
```

Understanding Vector Assets

Vector assets are XML-based images that scale without losing quality. They are excellent for icons, simple shapes, and scalable objects in your game.

Advantages of Vector Assets

1. **Scalability**: Maintain quality regardless of size.
2. **Smaller file size**: Especially for simple designs.
3. **Lightweight rendering**: Ideal for mobile games.

Adding Vector Assets to Your Game

Step 1: Import a Vector Asset

1. Right-click on the `res/drawable` folder.
2. Select **New → Vector Asset**.
3. Choose an existing vector or import your SVG file.

For example, you might add a `player_icon.xml`.

Step 2: Use the Vector in Your Layout

Use the `<ImageView>` component in XML to display the vector.

xml

```
<ImageView

android:layout_width="100dp"
```

```
android:layout_height="100dp"

android:src="@drawable/player_icon"

android:contentDescription="Player Icon" />
```

Step 3: Draw the Vector Programmatically

You can also load and draw a vector programmatically with `VectorDrawableCompat`.

Kotlin

```
val vectorDrawable = AppCompatResources.getDrawable(context,
R.drawable.player_icon)
```

```
vectorDrawable?.setBounds(100
, 100, 300, 300)
vectorDrawable?.draw(canvas)
```

Using Bitmap and Vector Assets in Games

Let's create a small example where we load a bitmap as the background and a vector as the player's character.

Complete Example: Using Bitmap and Vector Assets

1. Add a `background.png` to the `drawable` folder.
2. Add a `player_icon.xml` vector asset.

Custom View Code
Kotlin

```kotlin
class GameView(context: Context) : View(context) {

    private val background: Bitmap = BitmapFactory.decodeResource(resources, R.drawable.background)
    private val playerDrawable = AppCompatResources.getDrawable(context, R.drawable.player_icon)

    override fun onDraw(canvas: Canvas) {
        super.onDraw(canvas)

        // Draw the background bitmap
```

```
canvas.drawBitmap(background, 0f, 0f, null)

        // Draw the player vector
        playerDrawable?.setBounds(100, 300, 200, 400)
        playerDrawable?.draw(canvas)
    }
}
```

Activity Code
Kotlin

```
class MainActivity : AppCompatActivity() {
```

```kotlin
    override fun onCreate(savedInstanceState: Bundle?) {

super.onCreate(savedInstanceState)

        // Set the custom GameView as the content view

setContentView(GameView(this))
    }
}
```

When you run this code, you'll see the bitmap background with the player icon drawn on top of it.

Tips for Efficient Asset Management

1. **Use the Right Format**:
   - Use **Bitmaps** for detailed images like game backgrounds.
   - Use **Vectors** for scalable assets like icons and simple shapes.
2. **Optimize Memory Usage**:
   - Avoid loading large bitmaps directly; resize or compress them.
   - Use caching for frequently accessed assets.
3. **Preload Assets**:
   - For smoother gameplay, preload assets during the loading screen or splash screen.

6.3 Animating Objects for Dynamic Gameplay

Animation is an essential aspect of modern game design. It adds movement, interaction, and vibrancy to the gameplay, transforming static elements into a dynamic experience. Whether it's animating a character running, objects moving across the screen, or creating visual effects like explosions, Android's tools make it straightforward to implement.

1. Principles of Game Animation

Animation in games can be classified into two main types:

- **Property Animations**: Modify the properties of objects like position, rotation, scale, or transparency over time. Android's `ObjectAnimator` class is commonly used for this.
- **Frame-Based Animations**: Custom, per-frame updates suitable for games that demand real-time changes.

A good animation should:

- **Be smooth**: Avoid jerky transitions.
- **Match the gameplay**: Reflect the style and mechanics of your game.
- **Balance performance**: Ensure animations don't overburden the device.

2. Using `ObjectAnimator` for Property Animations

The `ObjectAnimator` class is a powerful tool to animate properties of game elements. Let's start with a simple example: making a game object bounce.

Example: Animating a Bouncing Ball

1. Add a `ImageView` for the ball in your XML layout (`activity_main.xml`):

xml

```
<ImageView
    android:id="@+id/ball"

android:layout_width="50dp"

android:layout_height="50dp"

android:src="@drawable/ball"

android:layout_centerHorizontal="true"

android:layout_marginTop="100dp" />
```

2. Use `ObjectAnimator` to make the ball bounce vertically.

Kotlin

```kotlin
class MainActivity : AppCompatActivity() {
    override fun onCreate(savedInstanceState: Bundle?) {

        super.onCreate(savedInstanceState)

        setContentView(R.layout.activity_main)

        // Find the ball
        val ball = findViewById<ImageView>(R.id.ball)

        // Create an ObjectAnimator for vertical movement
```

```kotlin
        val bounceAnimator = ObjectAnimator.ofFloat(ball, "translationY", 0f, 500f)

bounceAnimator.duration = 1000 // Duration of each bounce

bounceAnimator.repeatCount = ValueAnimator.INFINITE // Infinite bounces

bounceAnimator.repeatMode = ValueAnimator.REVERSE // Reverse direction on repeat

bounceAnimator.start()
    }
}
```

This code animates the ball to move up and down repeatedly.

3. Frame-Based Animation for Dynamic Gameplay

For real-time, physics-based games, frame-based animation is often the better choice. This involves updating an object's position and properties at every frame.

Example: Animating a Ball with Frame-Based Animation

1. Create a custom `GameView`:

Kotlin

```
class GameView(context: Context) : View(context) {
```

```kotlin
    private val ballPaint = Paint().apply { color = Color.RED }
    private var ballX = 100f
    private var ballY = 100f
    private val ballRadius = 50f
    private var velocityX = 5f
    private var velocityY = 7f

    override fun onDraw(canvas: Canvas) {
        super.onDraw(canvas)

        // Draw the ball
        canvas.drawCircle(ballX, ballY, ballRadius, ballPaint)
```

```
// Update the ball's position
ballX += velocityX
ballY += velocityY

// Bounce off edges
if (ballX <= ballRadius || ballX >= width - ballRadius) velocityX = -velocityX
if (ballY <= ballRadius || ballY >= height - ballRadius) velocityY = -velocityY

// Redraw for the next frame
invalidate()
    }
}
```

2. Set this custom GameView as the activity's content:

Kotlin

```
class MainActivity : AppCompatActivity() {
    override fun onCreate(savedInstanceState: Bundle?) {
        super.onCreate(savedInstanceState)
        // Use the custom GameView
        setContentView(GameView(this))
    }
}
```

This creates a ball that bounces dynamically across the screen. The `invalidate()` method ensures the `onDraw()` method is repeatedly called to animate the ball.

4. Animating Game Characters with Sprite Sheets

Sprites are essential for character animations in games. A sprite sheet contains frames of a character's animation sequence.

Example: Animating a Running Character

1. Create a `Bitmap` sprite sheet (e.g., `character_sprites.png`) containing frames of a running animation.
2. Add the sprite sheet to your project and use the following code to animate it:

Kotlin

```kotlin
class SpriteAnimationView(context: Context) : View(context) {

    private val spriteSheet = BitmapFactory.decodeResource(resources, R.drawable.character_sprites)
    private val frameWidth = spriteSheet.width / 4  // Assume 4 frames horizontally
    private val frameHeight = spriteSheet.height
    private var currentFrame = 0
    private val framePaint = Paint()

    override fun onDraw(canvas: Canvas) {
```

```
super.onDraw(canvas)

    // Calculate the source rectangle for the current frame
    val srcRect = Rect(currentFrame * frameWidth, 0, (currentFrame + 1) * frameWidth, frameHeight)
    val dstRect = Rect(100, 100, 300, 300) // Destination rectangle on the screen

    // Draw the current frame
    canvas.drawBitmap(spriteSheet, srcRect, dstRect, framePaint)
```

```
        // Update the frame
        currentFrame            =
(currentFrame + 1) % 4      //
Loop through 4 frames

        //   Redraw   for  the
next frame
postInvalidateDelayed(100)
// Delay for smooth animation
    }
}
```

3. Use this custom view in your activity:

Kotlin

```
class       MainActivity      :
AppCompatActivity() {
    override            fun
onCreate(savedInstanceState:
Bundle?) {
```

```
super.onCreate(savedInstanceS
tate)

setContentView(SpriteAnimatio
nView(this))
    }
}
```

This code creates a smooth, looping animation of a character running.

5. Integrating Animations into Game Mechanics

Animations should enhance gameplay, not just aesthetics. For example:

- **Visual feedback**: Animate a button press or explosion to signal user action.

- **Game events**: Show animations when the player scores or loses.

Example: Exploding Effect on Collision

When a ball hits a target, you can animate an explosion effect:

1. Use a particle animation library or create a custom effect using multiple small circles.
2. Trigger the animation on collision detection.

---

6. Tips for Smooth Animations

- **Use Hardware Acceleration**: Ensure animations leverage the GPU for performance.
- **Reduce Overhead**: Keep animations lightweight to avoid frame drops.

- **Test on Devices**: Check animations on various screen sizes and refresh rates.

Project: Add Animation to Your "Catch the Ball" Game

Animations add depth and excitement to your game, making it more engaging and visually appealing. In this project, we will extend our "Catch the Ball" game by incorporating animations for the ball and game elements. Specifically, we will:

1. Animate the ball's movement for a realistic effect.
2. Add visual feedback like scaling and color changes when a ball is caught.
3. Implement particle effects for a rewarding experience when the player scores.

This project will elevate your game from basic functionality to a polished product with lively animations.

Step 1: Setting Up the Project

Before we start, ensure you have the completed "Catch the Ball" game from Chapter 5. Open your project in Android Studio.

Step 2: Adding Ball Movement Animation

We'll use Android's `ObjectAnimator` to smooth out the ball's movement and make it feel more realistic.

Code: Animating the Ball's Fall

1. **Update the Ball's Properties**
   Open `GameView` and modify the ball's falling behavior:

Kotlin

```kotlin
import android.animation.ObjectAnimator

import android.animation.ValueAnimator

import android.graphics.Canvas

import android.graphics.Color

import android.graphics.Paint

import android.view.View


class GameView(context: Context) : View(context) {
```

```kotlin
    private val ballPaint = Paint().apply { color = Color.RED }
    private var ballX = 300f
    private var ballY = 0f
    private val ballRadius = 50f
    private var fallingAnimator: ObjectAnimator? = null

    init {
        // Start ball animation
        startBallAnimation()
    }
```

```kotlin
private fun startBallAnimation() {
    fallingAnimator = ObjectAnimator.ofFloat(this, "ballY", 0f, height.toFloat())

    fallingAnimator?.apply {
        duration = 2000 // Ball takes 2 seconds to fall
        repeatCount = ValueAnimator.INFINITE
        repeatMode = ValueAnimator.RESTART
        start()
```

```kotlin
        }
    }


    // Property to update ball's Y-coordinate
    var ballYPosition: Float
        get() = ballY
        set(value) {
            ballY = value
            invalidate() // Redraw the screen
        }


    override fun onDraw(canvas: Canvas) {
```

```kotlin
        super.onDraw(canvas)

        // Draw the ball
        canvas.drawCircle(ballX, ballY, ballRadius, ballPaint)
    }

    override fun onDetachedFromWindow() {
        super.onDetachedFromWindow()
        fallingAnimator?.cancel()
    }
}
```

Explanation:

- `ObjectAnimator`: Smoothly animates the `ballY` property.
- `repeatCount`: Ensures the animation restarts infinitely.
- `invalidate()`: Triggers the `onDraw()` method to update the ball's position.

Step 3: Adding Visual Feedback on Ball Catch

When the ball is caught, we'll add animations to scale the ball and briefly change its color to reward the player.

Code: Ball Catch Feedback

1. Detect ball catch in your game logic and apply animations:

Kotlin

```kotlin
private fun onBallCaught() {
    // Animate ball scaling
    val scaleAnimator = ObjectAnimator.ofFloat(this, "scaleX", 1f, 1.5f, 1f)
    scaleAnimator.duration = 300


    // Animate color change
    ballPaint.color = Color.GREEN
```

```
    postDelayed({
ballPaint.color = Color.RED
}, 300)


    scaleAnimator.start()


    // Reset the ball position

    ballY = 0f

    invalidate()

}
```

Explanation:

- `scaleX`: Temporarily enlarges the ball for visual emphasis.

- `postDelayed`: Resets the ball's color after the animation.

Step 4: Adding Particle Effects for Scoring

Particle effects provide a visually satisfying way to celebrate scoring points. Here, we'll create a simple particle system.

Code: Particle Effect Implementation

1. Add a `Particle` class to represent individual particles:

Kotlin

```
data class Particle(
    var x: Float,
```

```kotlin
    var y: Float,
    val dx: Float,
    val dy: Float,
    val color: Int,
    var life: Int
)
```

2. Create a particle system in `GameView`:

Kotlin

```kotlin
private val particles = mutableListOf<Particle>()
private val particlePaint = Paint()
```

```kotlin
private fun createParticles(x: Float, y: Float) {
    for (i in 0..20) {
        val dx = (-5..5).random().toFloat()
        val dy = (-5..5).random().toFloat()
        val color = Color.rgb((0..255).random(), (0..255).random(), (0..255).random())

        particles.add(Particle(x, y, dx, dy, color, 50))
    }
}
```

```
private fun updateParticles()
{
    val iterator = particles.iterator()
    while (iterator.hasNext()) {
        val particle = iterator.next()
        particle.x += particle.dx
        particle.y += particle.dy
        particle.life--

        if (particle.life <= 0) iterator.remove()
```

        }

}

3. Draw the particles in onDraw():

Kotlin

```
override fun onDraw(canvas: Canvas) {

    super.onDraw(canvas)


    // Draw the ball

    canvas.drawCircle(ballX, ballY, ballRadius, ballPaint)


    // Draw particles
```

```
    for (particle in particles) {
        particlePaint.color = particle.color

canvas.drawCircle(particle.x, particle.y,           10f, particlePaint)

    }


    // Update particle positions
    updateParticles()
}
```

4. Trigger particle effects when the ball is caught:

Kotlin

```
private fun onBallCaught() {
    createParticles(ballX, ballY)
    // Existing animations and reset logic...
}
```

Step 5: Refining the Gameplay Experience

Here are a few tips to ensure the animations enhance the game:

- **Timing**: Adjust animation durations to match the game's pace.

- **Feedback Loop**: Provide instant visual or audio feedback for all interactions.
- **Testing**: Test animations on various devices to ensure smooth performance.

Step 6: Running the Enhanced Game

Run your project and enjoy the dynamic, animated experience:

1. The ball falls smoothly with `ObjectAnimator`.
2. When caught, it scales up briefly and changes color.
3. Particle effects explode at the catch location, creating a rewarding visual.

Part 3:
Advanced Game Development Techniques

Chapter 7: Building More Complex Games

Creating more complex games requires managing multiple elements like levels, game states, advanced input handling, and introducing dynamic features like power-ups, enemies, and scoring systems. This chapter guides you step-by-step through these concepts and helps you integrate them into your games.

7.1 Managing Multiple Levels and Game States

Managing multiple levels and game states is an essential skill for creating engaging games. A well-structured system for handling these elements ensures smooth transitions and a cohesive player experience. In this chapter, we'll explore how to design and implement these systems effectively.

What Are Game States?

Game states represent the different phases of your game, such as:

- **Main Menu**: The starting screen of the game.
- **Gameplay**: The active playing state.
- **Pause**: A temporary break in gameplay.
- **Game Over**: A state after losing the game.

Each state requires unique logic and user interactions, which we'll organize systematically.

Implementing Game States

We'll use an **enumeration (enum)** to define the possible states and handle them in the game loop.

Step 1: Define the Game States

Create an enum to represent each game state.

Kotlin

```kotlin
enum class GameState {
    MAIN_MENU,
    GAME_PLAY,
    PAUSED,
    GAME_OVER
}
```

Step 2: Set Up a Basic Game Structure

In your game class, create a variable to track the current game state.

Kotlin

```
class GameView(context: Context) : View(context) {

    private var currentGameState = GameState.MAIN_MENU

    override fun onDraw(canvas: Canvas) {
        super.onDraw(canvas)
```

```
        // Render different elements based on the game state
        when (currentGameState) {

GameState.MAIN_MENU        -> drawMainMenu(canvas)

GameState.GAME_PLAY        -> drawGameplay(canvas)

            GameState.PAUSED -> drawPauseScreen(canvas)

GameState.GAME_OVER        -> drawGameOverScreen(canvas)

        }
```

}

```kotlin
private fun drawMainMenu(canvas: Canvas) {
    // Draw main menu UI
    val paint = Paint()
    paint.textSize = 60f
    paint.color = Color.BLACK
    canvas.drawText("Main Menu - Tap to Play", 100f, 300f, paint)
}
```

```kotlin
    private fun drawGameplay(canvas: Canvas) {
        // Draw game elements
        canvas.drawColor(Color.WHITE) // Gameplay background
        // Additional gameplay drawing logic here
    }


    private fun drawPauseScreen(canvas: Canvas) {
        val paint = Paint()
        paint.textSize = 60f
```

```kotlin
        paint.color = Color.BLUE

        canvas.drawText("Game Paused", 100f, 300f, paint)

    }


    private fun drawGameOverScreen(canvas: Canvas) {

        val paint = Paint()

        paint.textSize = 60f

        paint.color = Color.RED

        canvas.drawText("Game Over", 100f, 300f, paint)

    }
```

}

Step 3: Transition Between States

Handle state changes using user input, such as taps or gestures.

Kotlin

```
override                          fun
onTouchEvent(event:
MotionEvent): Boolean {

    if    (event.action    ==
MotionEvent.ACTION_DOWN) {

        when
(currentGameState) {
```

```
GameState.MAIN_MENU -> {

    currentGameState =
    GameState.GAME_PLAY

}

GameState.GAME_PLAY -> {

    currentGameState =
    GameState.PAUSED

}

         GameState.PAUSED
-> {

    currentGameState =
    GameState.GAME_PLAY
```

```
            }

GameState.GAME_OVER -> {

currentGameState                =
GameState.MAIN_MENU

            }
        }

        invalidate()       //
Redraw  the  screen  with  the
new state

    }

    return true

}
```

What Are Levels?

Levels are unique stages of the game, each with distinct challenges, layouts, and objectives. Managing levels involves:

1. **Loading Resources**: Assets like images and sounds specific to each level.
2. **Designing Layouts**: Different obstacle or platform arrangements for each level.
3. **Transitioning**: Smoothly moving between levels.

Implementing Levels

Step 1: Create a Level Manager

A `LevelManager` helps organize levels.

Kotlin

```
class LevelManager {
```

```kotlin
    private var currentLevel = 1

    fun loadLevel(level: Int) {
        currentLevel = level
        // Load level-specific assets and configurations
    }

    fun nextLevel() {
        currentLevel++
        loadLevel(currentLevel)
    }
```

```kotlin
    fun getCurrentLevel(): Int {
        return currentLevel
    }
}
```

Step 2: Integrate Levels into the Game

Update the `GameView` to use the `LevelManager`.

Kotlin

```kotlin
private val levelManager = LevelManager()
```

```kotlin
private fun drawGameplay(canvas: Canvas) {

canvas.drawColor(Color.LTGRAY) // Level background

    val paint = Paint()

    paint.textSize = 40f

    paint.color = Color.BLACK

    canvas.drawText("Level: ${levelManager.getCurrentLevel()}", 100f, 100f, paint)


    // Add level-specific drawing logic here

}
```

Step 3: Level Transitions

Move to the next level after completing the current one.

Kotlin

```kotlin
fun completeLevel() {
    if (levelManager.getCurrentLevel() == MAX_LEVEL) {
        currentGameState = GameState.GAME_OVER
    } else {

levelManager.nextLevel()
```

```
            invalidate()

    }

}
```

Practical Example: Switching Between Levels and States

Here's how the game might flow:

1. Start at the **Main Menu**.
2. Tap to transition to **Game Play**.
3. `Complete Level 1 → Transition to Level 2`.
4. Pause or resume gameplay at any point.
5. `Reach the final level → Transition to` **Game Over**.

Challenges in Managing Levels and States

- **Complex Logic**: As levels increase, transitions and resource management become intricate.
- **Memory Management**: Efficiently load and unload level-specific assets.
- **Player Experience**: Ensure smooth transitions and intuitive controls.

7.2 Advanced Input Handling (Gestures, Multi-Touch, etc.)

When building mobile games, handling player input in an intuitive way is crucial to creating an engaging and responsive experience. In this chapter, we'll cover advanced input handling techniques, including **gestures**, **multi-touch**, and **other user interactions** that can significantly enhance gameplay. By the end of this chapter, you'll have a solid understanding of how to use these techniques to create dynamic, interactive mobile games.

What Is Advanced Input Handling?

Advanced input handling goes beyond basic touch interactions and allows for more complex control schemes. These include:

- **Gestures**: Swipes, pinches, and other touch-based movements.
- **Multi-Touch**: Detecting multiple touch points simultaneously, useful for games requiring two-handed or multi-finger interactions.
- **Custom Input Events**: Handling different input events like drag, pinch zoom, or rotation.

In Android, these input techniques are handled using `GestureDetector`, `ScaleGestureDetector`, and direct access to `MotionEvent` for fine-grained control.

Gestures in Android

Android provides a built-in mechanism to handle common gestures like swipes, long presses, and double taps using `GestureDetector`. It simplifies gesture recognition and allows for easy integration into your game.

Step 1: Setting Up Gesture Detection

First, let's initialize the `GestureDetector` to detect swipes and other gestures.

Kotlin

```kotlin
class GameView(context: Context) : View(context), GestureDetector.OnGestureListener {

    private val gestureDetector: GestureDetector = GestureDetector(context, this)


    override fun onTouchEvent(event: MotionEvent): Boolean {

        gestureDetector.onTouchEvent(event) // Pass the touch event to the GestureDetector
```

        return true

    }

    // Implement required methods for gesture detection

    override fun onDown(e: MotionEvent?): Boolean {

        // Handle initial touch down event

        return true

    }

    override fun onFling(e1: MotionEvent?, e2: MotionEvent?, velocityX:

```kotlin
Float, velocityY: Float): Boolean {

    // Handle swipe fling

    if (velocityX > 0) {

        // Swipe right action

    } else {

        // Swipe left action

    }

    return true

}


override fun onScroll(e1: MotionEvent?, e2: MotionEvent?, distanceX:
```

```kotlin
Float, distanceY: Float): Boolean {
    // Handle scroll gesture (e.g., dragging)
    return true
}

override fun onLongPress(e: MotionEvent?) {
    // Handle long press gesture (e.g., a prolonged tap)
}
```

```kotlin
override fun onShowPress(e: MotionEvent?) {
    // Handle short press without releasing
}


override fun onSingleTapUp(e: MotionEvent?): Boolean {
    // Handle single tap release
    return true
}
```

```kotlin
    override fun onDoubleTap(e: MotionEvent?): Boolean {
        // Handle double tap
        return true
    }

    override fun onDoubleTapEvent(e: MotionEvent?): Boolean {
        // Handle ongoing double tap event
        return true
    }
}
```

Here, we implement a `GestureDetector.OnGestureListener` to detect different gestures such as swipes and taps. The `onTouchEvent()` method passes touch events to the `GestureDetector`, which then processes them based on the gesture.

Step 2: Handling Different Gestures

Each method of the `GestureDetector.OnGestureListener` corresponds to a specific gesture:

- `onDown()`: Triggered when the user first touches the screen.
- `onFling()`: Called when a user swipes or flings across the screen.
- `onScroll()`: Triggered when the user drags their finger across the screen.

- `onLongPress()`: Triggered by a long press on the screen.
- `onSingleTapUp()`: Triggered by a tap (when the finger is released).
- `onDoubleTap()`: Triggered by a double tap.

For example, if you want to detect a swipe gesture to move an object in your game:

Kotlin

```
override fun onFling(e1: MotionEvent?, e2: MotionEvent?, velocityX: Float, velocityY: Float): Boolean {
    if (velocityX > 0) {
        // Move the player or object to the right
```

```
        player.x += 10

    } else {

        // Move the player or object to the left

        player.x -= 10

    }

    return true

}
```

Multi-Touch Input

Multi-touch input is important for games that require complex controls, such as zooming, rotating, or using both hands simultaneously. Android provides a `MotionEvent` object that contains the positions of all active touch points on the screen.

Step 1: Detecting Multiple Touch Points

We can detect multiple touch events using the `MotionEvent` object's `getPointerCount()` and `getPointerId()` methods. For example, if you want to implement a two-finger pinch zoom, you can use this code:

Kotlin

```
override fun onTouchEvent(event: MotionEvent): Boolean {
    when (event.actionMasked) {
```

```
MotionEvent.ACTION_POINTER_DOWN -> {
    val pointerIndex = event.actionIndex
    val pointerId = event.getPointerId(pointerIndex)
    // Handle a new touch point (e.g., two-finger pinch)
}

MotionEvent.ACTION_MOVE -> {
    val pointerCount = event.pointerCount
    if (pointerCount == 2) {
```

```
            // Calculate distance between two touch points for pinch zoom
            val dx = event.getX(0) - event.getX(1)
            val dy = event.getY(0) - event.getY(1)
            val distance = Math.sqrt((dx * dx + dy * dy).toDouble())

handlePinchZoom(distance.toFloat())
        }
    }

MotionEvent.ACTION_UP,
```

```
MotionEvent.ACTION_POINTER_UP
-> {
            // Handle finger release
        }
    }
    return true
}
```

In the code above, `ACTION_POINTER_DOWN` detects when a new finger touches the screen. We use `getPointerCount()` and `getX()/getY()` for multi-touch interaction. The `ACTION_MOVE` event is used to track the movement of the fingers.

Step 2: Pinch to Zoom

For a pinch-to-zoom interaction, we calculate the distance between two touch points, and if the distance changes, we adjust the scale of the object.

Kotlin

```
private var initialDistance: Float = 0f


private fun handlePinchZoom(currentDistance: Float) {
    if (initialDistance == 0f) {
        initialDistance = currentDistance
```

```
} else {
    val scale = currentDistance / initialDistance
    // Adjust the scale of the object
    gameObject.scale(scale)
    }
}
```

Here, we compute the difference in distance between the two fingers (`currentDistance - initialDistance`) and use this value to scale an object in the game accordingly.

Advanced Gesture Handling: Swipe, Drag, and Rotation

While `GestureDetector` handles simple gestures, you may want to create custom gestures like drag-and-drop or rotation. Here's how you can handle these more complex interactions.

Kotlin

```
private var lastX: Float = 0f
private var lastY: Float = 0f


override fun onScroll(e1: MotionEvent?, e2: MotionEvent?, distanceX: Float, distanceY: Float): Boolean {
```

```
    // Implement custom dragging functionality
    if (e2 != null) {
        val deltaX = e2.x - lastX
        val deltaY = e2.y - lastY
        // Move an object based on the difference in touch coordinates
        gameObject.x += deltaX
        gameObject.y += deltaY
    }
    lastX = e2?.x ?: 0f
    lastY = e2?.y ?: 0f
```

```
        return true

}
```

This method is great for dragging objects around on the screen. We keep track of the previous touch position (`lastX`, `lastY`) and compute the difference from the current touch to update the position of the object.

7.3 Adding Power-Ups, Enemies, and Scoring

Enhancing a game with power-ups, enemies, and a scoring system makes gameplay more engaging and provides players with goals and challenges. In this chapter, we'll guide you through implementing these features step by step, with practical examples to help you integrate them into your game. By the end, you'll have a framework to build more dynamic and rewarding gameplay experiences.

Power-Ups

Power-ups are temporary boosts or abilities that enhance the player's performance. Examples include speed boosts, invincibility, or additional points.

Step 1: Designing Power-Ups

Start by defining what your power-ups will do. For instance:

- **Speed Boost**: Temporarily increases player movement speed.
- **Shield**: Protects the player from one hit.

- **Bonus Points**: Adds extra points to the score.

Step 2: Representing Power-Ups in Code

Create a `PowerUp` class to handle power-up properties and behavior.

Kotlin

```kotlin
data class PowerUp(
    val type: String, // Type of power-up (e.g., "speed", "shield", "points")
    var x: Float,     // X position
    var y: Float,     // Y position
```

```
    var isActive: Boolean = true // Indicates if the power-up is still active
)
```

Step 3: Spawning Power-Ups

Periodically spawn power-ups at random positions on the screen. For example:

Kotlin

```
val powerUps = mutableListOf<PowerUp>()

fun spawnPowerUp() {
```

```
    val types =
listOf("speed", "shield",
"points")

    val randomType =
types.random()

    val randomX =
(Math.random() *
screenWidth).toFloat()

    val randomY =
(Math.random() *
screenHeight).toFloat()


powerUps.add(PowerUp(randomTy
pe, randomX, randomY))

    }
```

Step 4: Collecting Power-Ups

Detect collision between the player and a power-up to activate it.

Kotlin

```
fun checkPowerUpCollision(player: Player) {
    for (powerUp in powerUps) {
        if (powerUp.isActive && isColliding(player.x, player.y, powerUp.x, powerUp.y)) {

activatePowerUp(powerUp)
```

```
            powerUp.isActive = false // Remove the power-up after use
        }
    }
}


fun activatePowerUp(powerUp: PowerUp) {
    when (powerUp.type) {
        "speed" -> player.speed *= 2
        "shield" -> player.hasShield = true
        "points" -> score += 50
```

```
        }
}
```

The `isColliding()` function checks if the player intersects with the power-up, and `activatePowerUp()` applies the effect.

Enemies

Enemies create obstacles for players and add a challenge to the game.

Step 1: Creating an Enemy Class

Define properties and behavior for enemies.

Kotlin

```
data class Enemy(
    var x: Float,
    var y: Float,
    val speed: Float
)


val enemies = mutableListOf<Enemy>()
```

Step 2: Spawning Enemies

Spawn enemies at intervals with random starting positions.

Kotlin

```kotlin
fun spawnEnemy() {
    val randomX = (Math.random() * screenWidth).toFloat()
    val randomSpeed = (3..7).random().toFloat()

    enemies.add(Enemy(randomX, 0f, randomSpeed))
}
```

Step 3: Moving Enemies

Update enemy positions during the game loop.

Kotlin

```
fun moveEnemies() {
    for (enemy in enemies) {
        enemy.y += enemy.speed
        if (enemy.y > screenHeight) {
enemies.remove(enemy) // Remove enemies that go off-screen
        }
    }
}
```

Step 4: Detecting Collisions

Check for collisions between enemies and the player.

Kotlin

```kotlin
fun checkEnemyCollisions(player: Player) {
    for (enemy in enemies) {
        if (isColliding(player.x, player.y, enemy.x, enemy.y)) {
            if (player.hasShield) {
```

```
            player.hasShield = false //
Shield absorbs the hit
                } else {
                    player.lives
-= 1 // Reduce player lives
                }
            }
        }
}
```

Scoring System

A scoring system provides feedback and motivation for players.

Step 1: Tracking the Score

Add a score variable and initialize it.

Kotlin

```kotlin
var score = 0
```

Step 2: Incrementing the Score

Increase the score when the player performs specific actions, such as collecting items or avoiding enemies.

Kotlin

```kotlin
fun updateScore() {
    score += 1 // Increment score as time passes
}
```

Step 3: Displaying the Score

Render the score on the screen.

Kotlin

```kotlin
fun drawScore(canvas: Canvas, paint: Paint) {
    paint.color = Color.WHITE
    paint.textSize = 50f
    canvas.drawText("Score: $score", 20f, 50f, paint)
```

}

Step 4: Adding Bonus Points

Award bonus points when specific conditions are met.

Kotlin

```
if (player.collectsPowerUp("points")) {
    score += 50
}
```

Integrating Power-Ups, Enemies, and Scoring

Let's bring it all together in the game loop:

Kotlin

```
override fun onDraw(canvas: Canvas) {
    super.onDraw(canvas)

    // Spawn power-ups and enemies
    if (System.currentTimeMillis() % 5000L == 0L) spawnPowerUp()
```

```
    if (System.currentTimeMillis() % 3000L == 0L) spawnEnemy()

    // Update and draw power-ups
    for (powerUp in powerUps) {
        if (powerUp.isActive) drawPowerUp(canvas, powerUp)
    }


    // Update and draw enemies
    moveEnemies()
    for (enemy in enemies) {
```

```
        drawEnemy(canvas, enemy)
    }

    // Check collisions
    checkPowerUpCollision(player)
    checkEnemyCollisions(player)

    // Update score and lives
    updateScore()
    drawScore(canvas, paint)
    drawPlayerLives(canvas, paint, player)
```

```
    // Draw player
    drawPlayer(canvas, 
player)


    invalidate()   // Redraw 
the screen
}
```

Project: Develop a Multi-Level Platformer Game

Creating a multi-level platformer game is a fun way to combine everything you've learned so far, from basic game mechanics to animation and collision handling. In this project, you'll design a game where the player progresses through multiple levels, facing new challenges and increasingly complex obstacles. This chapter will guide you step by step to build your own multi-level platformer game.

Step 1: Game Design Overview

Before coding, let's outline the key components of our platformer game:

1. **Player**: A character controlled by the user.
2. **Platforms**: Surfaces the player can jump on to reach the goal.
3. **Enemies**: Moving obstacles that reduce player lives on contact.
4. **Power-Ups**: Optional boosts, such as extra points or invincibility.
5. **Levels**: Multiple stages with increasing difficulty.

6. **Goal**: A target the player must reach to complete the level.

Step 2: Setting Up the Game Structure

Let's start by defining the game's main components.

Class Definitions

Kotlin

```kotlin
// Player class
data class Player(
    var x: Float,
    var y: Float,
    var speedX: Float = 0f,
```

```kotlin
    var speedY: Float = 0f,

    var isJumping: Boolean = false,

    var lives: Int = 3
)


// Platform class
data class Platform(
    var x: Float,
    var y: Float,
    val width: Float,
    val height: Float
)
```

```kotlin
// Enemy class
data class Enemy(
    var x: Float,
    var y: Float,
    val speed: Float
)

// Goal class
data class Goal(
    var x: Float,
    var y: Float
)

// Level class
```

```kotlin
data class Level(
    val platforms: List<Platform>,
    val enemies: List<Enemy>,
    val goal: Goal
)
```

Step 3: Building Levels

Design levels with varying layouts, using platforms, enemies, and goals.

Level 1 Example

Kotlin

```kotlin
val level1 = Level(
```

```
    platforms = listOf(
        Platform(50f,   400f, 200f, 20f),
        Platform(300f,  300f, 150f, 20f),
        Platform(500f,  200f, 200f, 20f)
    ),
    enemies = listOf(
        Enemy(350f,   270f, 2f),
        Enemy(550f, 170f, 3f)
    ),
    goal = Goal(700f, 150f)
)
```

Level 2 Example

Kotlin

```kotlin
val level2 = Level(
    platforms = listOf(
        Platform(100f, 450f, 250f, 20f),
        Platform(400f, 350f, 150f, 20f),
        Platform(650f, 250f, 200f, 20f)
    ),
    enemies = listOf(
```

```
        Enemy(450f,      330f, 3f),
        Enemy(700f, 230f, 4f)
    ),
    goal = Goal(850f, 200f)
)
)
```

Step 4: Implementing Core Mechanics

Platform Collision Detection

Ensure the player doesn't fall through platforms or pass through them.

Kotlin

```
fun
checkPlatformCollision(player
:      Player,    platforms:
List<Platform>) {

    for    (platform    in
platforms) {

        if    (player.y    +
PLAYER_HEIGHT   >=   platform.y
&&

            player.y        +
PLAYER_HEIGHT <= platform.y +
platform.height &&

            player.x        +
PLAYER_WIDTH >= platform.x &&

            player.x        <=
platform.x + platform.width)
{
```

```
                player.isJumping = false
                player.speedY = 0f
                player.y = platform.y - PLAYER_HEIGHT // Align player to platform top
            }
        }
    }
}
```

Enemy Interaction

Reduce lives if the player touches an enemy.

Kotlin

```
fun checkEnemyCollision(player: Player, enemies: List<Enemy>) {
    for (enemy in enemies) {
        if (isColliding(player.x, player.y, enemy.x, enemy.y)) {
            player.lives -= 1
            if (player.lives <= 0) {
                gameOver()
            }
        }
    }
}
```

Level Completion

Check if the player reaches the goal.

Kotlin

```kotlin
fun checkGoalReached(player: Player, goal: Goal): Boolean {
    return isColliding(player.x, player.y, goal.x, goal.y)
}
```

Step 5: Adding Player Movement

Allow the player to move left, right, and jump.

Kotlin

```kotlin
fun updatePlayerPosition(player: Player) {
    // Apply horizontal movement
    player.x += player.speedX

    // Apply gravity for vertical movement
    if (player.isJumping) {
        player.speedY += GRAVITY
    }
```

```
    player.y += player.speedY


    // Limit player position within screen bounds
    player.x = player.x.coerceIn(0f, screenWidth - PLAYER_WIDTH)

    player.y = player.y.coerceIn(0f, screenHeight - PLAYER_HEIGHT)
}


// Jumping
fun jump(player: Player) {
    if (!player.isJumping) {
```

```
        player.isJumping =
true
        player.speedY = -15f
// Jump force
    }
}
```

Step 6: Rendering Graphics

Drawing Platforms, Enemies, and Goal

Render each component during the game loop.

Kotlin

```
fun drawPlatforms(canvas: Canvas, platforms:
```

```
List<Platform>, paint: Paint) 
{

    paint.color = Color.GRAY

    for (platform in platforms) {


canvas.drawRect(platform.x, platform.y, platform.x + platform.width, platform.y + platform.height, paint)

    }
}


fun drawEnemies(canvas: Canvas, enemies: List<Enemy>, paint: Paint) {

    paint.color = Color.RED
```

```
    for (enemy in enemies) {

canvas.drawCircle(enemy.x, enemy.y, 20f, paint)

        }
}


fun drawGoal(canvas: Canvas, goal: Goal, paint: Paint) {

    paint.color = Color.YELLOW

    canvas.drawCircle(goal.x, goal.y, 30f, paint)

}
```

Step 7: Adding Levels

Progress to the next level when the player reaches the goal.

Kotlin

```
var currentLevelIndex = 0
val levels = listOf(level1, level2)

fun nextLevel() {
    if (currentLevelIndex < levels.size - 1) {
        currentLevelIndex += 1
```

```
loadLevel(levels[currentLevel
Index])

    } else {

        showVictoryScreen()

    }

}
```

Step 8: The Game Loop

Bring everything together in the `onDraw` method.

Kotlin

```kotlin
override fun onDraw(canvas: Canvas) {
    super.onDraw(canvas)

    val currentLevel = levels[currentLevelIndex]
    // Draw platforms, enemies, and goal
    drawPlatforms(canvas, currentLevel.platforms, paint)
    drawEnemies(canvas, currentLevel.enemies, paint)
    drawGoal(canvas, currentLevel.goal, paint)

    // Update player position
```

```
updatePlayerPosition(player)

checkPlatformCollision(player
, currentLevel.platforms)

checkEnemyCollision(player,
currentLevel.enemies)

    // Check if goal is reached
    if (checkGoalReached(player,
currentLevel.goal)) {
        nextLevel()
    }
```

```
    // Draw player
    drawPlayer(canvas, player)

    // Refresh screen
    invalidate()
}
```

This chapter introduced techniques for creating more sophisticated games. By managing levels, handling advanced input, and adding engaging features like enemies and scoring, you're now ready to design games that challenge and delight players. Let your creativity run wild as you experiment with these features!

Chapter 8: Integrating Sound and Music

Sound and music are vital for enhancing the immersion and engagement of your game. A well-designed audio experience can amplify excitement, create atmosphere, and provide critical feedback to players. This chapter will walk you through integrating background music, sound effects, and efficient audio resource management in your Android game.

8.1 Adding Background Music and Sound Effects

Audio plays a critical role in shaping the player's experience in a game. Background music can set the atmosphere, while sound effects provide feedback and immersion. This section will guide you through integrating background music and sound effects into your

Android game using Kotlin. By the end, your game will come alive with engaging audio elements.

Understanding Android's Audio Framework

Android offers two primary tools for integrating sound:

1. **MediaPlayer**: Best for long-running audio, such as background music.
2. **SoundPool**: Ideal for short and quick-play sounds, like effects for jumps or collisions.

We'll explore both, demonstrating how to use them effectively in your game.

Adding Background Music with `MediaPlayer`

The `MediaPlayer` class is designed for playing longer audio files, such as background music, with support for looping and control over playback.

Steps to Add Background Music

1. Add your audio file (e.g., `background_music.mp3`) to the `res/raw` folder in your Android project.
2. Use `MediaPlayer` to load, play, and manage the music.
3. Ensure proper handling of the `MediaPlayer` lifecycle to prevent memory leaks.

Example: Adding Background Music

Here's how to implement background music in your game:

Kotlin

```
// Declare MediaPlayer
private lateinit var backgroundMusic: MediaPlayer

override fun onCreate(savedInstanceState: Bundle?) {

super.onCreate(savedInstanceState)
```

```
setContentView(R.layout.activity_main)

    // Initialize MediaPlayer with background music
    backgroundMusic = MediaPlayer.create(this, R.raw.background_music)
    backgroundMusic.isLooping = true // Set music to loop
    backgroundMusic.start() // Start playback
}
```

```kotlin
// Stop and release the MediaPlayer when the activity is destroyed
override fun onDestroy() {
    super.onDestroy()
    if (this::backgroundMusic.isInitialized && backgroundMusic.isPlaying) {

        backgroundMusic.stop()     // Stop playback

        backgroundMusic.release()  // Release resources
    }
}
```

Adding Sound Effects with `SoundPool`

The `SoundPool` class is optimized for short, fast, and multiple concurrent sounds. It works well for effects like button clicks, collisions, and character actions.

Steps to Add Sound Effects

1. Place your sound effect files (e.g., `jump.wav`, `collision.wav`) in the `res/raw` folder.
2. Load the sounds into `SoundPool`.
3. Trigger playback when events occur in the game.

Example: Adding Sound Effects

Kotlin

```kotlin
// Declare SoundPool and sound IDs
private lateinit var soundPool: SoundPool
private var jumpSoundId: Int = 0
private var collisionSoundId: Int = 0


override fun onCreate(savedInstanceState: Bundle?) {
```

```
super.onCreate(savedInstanceState)

setContentView(R.layout.activity_main)

    // Initialize SoundPool
    soundPool = SoundPool.Builder()
        .setMaxStreams(5)  // Maximum number of simultaneous sounds
        .build()

    // Load sound effects
```

```
    jumpSoundId                =
soundPool.load(this,
R.raw.jump, 1)

    collisionSoundId           =
soundPool.load(this,
R.raw.collision, 1)

}


// Play sound effects on
specific game actions

fun playJumpSound() {

soundPool.play(jumpSoundId,
1f, 1f, 0, 0, 1f) // Volume
1.0, no loop

}
```

```kotlin
fun playCollisionSound() {

    soundPool.play(collisionSoundId, 1f, 1f, 0, 0, 1f)

}


// Release SoundPool resources when the activity is destroyed
override fun onDestroy() {
    super.onDestroy()
    soundPool.release()
}
```

Best Practices for Audio Integration

Volume Control: Allow players to adjust the volume of music and effects independently. Use sliders or settings menus for better UX.
Kotlin

```kotlin
fun setMusicVolume(volume: Float) {

backgroundMusic.setVolume(volume, volume) // Set left and right volume

}


fun setSoundEffectVolume(soundId: Int, volume: Float) {
```

```
soundPool.setVolume(soundId, 
volume, volume) // Set sound 
effect volume
```

}

1.

Lifecycle Management: Pause or resume audio during activity lifecycle events, such as when the app is minimized or resumed.
Kotlin

```
override fun onPause() {

    super.onPause()

    if 
(this::backgroundMusic.isInit
ialized                    && 
backgroundMusic.isPlaying) {
```

```kotlin
            backgroundMusic.pause()
        }
    }


    override fun onResume() {
        super.onResume()
        if (this::backgroundMusic.isInitialized             && !backgroundMusic.isPlaying) {
            backgroundMusic.start()
        }
    }
```

2.

3. **Optimize Resource Usage**:
    - Use compressed audio formats like `.ogg` or `.mp3` to reduce file sizes.
    - Avoid loading excessive sounds simultaneously to save memory.

Tips for Choosing Audio

- Select music that matches your game's theme (e.g., fast-paced tracks for action games, serene melodies for puzzles).
- Ensure sound effects are clear and recognizable but not overwhelming.

8.2 Managing Audio Resources Efficiently

Efficient audio management is essential for performance, especially on mobile devices with limited resources.

Avoid Overloading the System

- Limit the number of simultaneous sounds.
- Use compressed audio formats like `.ogg` or `.mp3` to reduce file size.

Pause and Resume Audio

Handle audio correctly during lifecycle events like pausing or resuming the game.

Code Example: Managing Audio During Lifecycle Events

override fun onPause() {

  super.onPause()

```
    if (backgroundMusic.isPlaying) {
        backgroundMusic.pause()    // Pause background music
    }
}

override fun onResume() {
    super.onResume()
    if (!backgroundMusic.isPlaying) {
        backgroundMusic.start()    // Resume background music
    }
}
```

Dynamic Volume Control

Allow players to adjust the volume of music and sound effects.

Code Example: Adjusting Volume Dynamically

```kotlin
fun setMusicVolume(volume: Float) {
    backgroundMusic.setVolume(volume, volume) // Adjust left and right channels
}

fun setSoundEffectVolume(soundId: Int, volume: Float) {
    soundPool.setVolume(soundId, volume, volume) // Adjust left and right channels
}
```

Project: Enhance Your Platformer Game with Sound Effects

Sound effects are a fantastic way to bring your platformer game to life. They enhance feedback for player actions, emphasize game events, and create an immersive experience. In this project, we'll integrate sound effects into your platformer game, focusing on adding audio for character actions, interactions, and game events.

By the end of this chapter, your platformer game will feel much more dynamic and engaging.

Step 1: Preparing Your Audio Files

Before we start coding, gather the audio files you'll use. For this project:

- **Jump Sound:** A sound effect for when the character jumps (e.g., `jump.wav`).
- **Coin Pickup Sound:** A sound effect for collecting coins or power-ups (e.g., `coin.wav`).
- **Game Over Sound:** A sound effect for the end of the game or losing a life (e.g., `game_over.wav`).

Place these files in the `res/raw` folder of your project.

Step 2: Setting Up SoundPool

We'll use `SoundPool` to handle sound effects efficiently. It's ideal for short and responsive audio.

Initialize SoundPool

In your game's activity, initialize a SoundPool instance and load your sound effects.

Kotlin

```
// Declare SoundPool and sound IDs
private lateinit var soundPool: SoundPool
private var jumpSoundId: Int = 0
private var coinSoundId: Int = 0
private var gameOverSoundId: Int = 0
```

```kotlin
override fun onCreate(savedInstanceState: Bundle?) {

super.onCreate(savedInstanceState)

setContentView(R.layout.activity_main)


    // Initialize SoundPool
    soundPool = SoundPool.Builder()
        .setMaxStreams(5) // Maximum simultaneous sounds
        .build()
```

```
    // Load sound effects
    jumpSoundId =
soundPool.load(this,
R.raw.jump, 1)
    coinSoundId =
soundPool.load(this,
R.raw.coin, 1)
    gameOverSoundId =
soundPool.load(this,
R.raw.game_over, 1)
}
```

Step 3: Integrating Sound Effects

Next, trigger the sound effects during game events.

Playing Jump Sound

Call the jump sound when the player character jumps.

Kotlin

```kotlin
fun playJumpSound() {

soundPool.play(jumpSoundId, 1f, 1f, 0, 0, 1f) // Full volume, no looping

}


// Example: Integrating in your jump action

fun onPlayerJump() {
```

```
    // Code for making the
character jump
    playJumpSound()  // Play
jump sound
}
```

Playing Coin Pickup Sound

Play the coin sound when the player collects a coin or power-up.

Kotlin

```
fun playCoinSound() {

soundPool.play(coinSoundId,
1f, 1f, 0, 0, 1f) // Full
volume, no looping
```

```
}

// Example: Triggering sound when a coin is collected

fun onCoinCollected() {
    // Code for updating score or coin count

    playCoinSound() // Play coin sound
}
```

Playing Game Over Sound

Play the game over sound when the player loses the game.

Kotlin

```kotlin
fun playGameOverSound() {

soundPool.play(gameOverSoundId, 1f, 1f, 0, 0, 1f) // Full volume, no looping

}


// Example: Triggering sound on game over
fun onGameOver() {
    // Code for ending the game
    playGameOverSound()   // Play game over sound
```

}

Step 4: Handling Volume and Lifecycle

Volume Control

Allow players to adjust sound effect volume using a settings menu or sliders.

Kotlin

```
fun setSoundEffectVolume(volume: Float) {

soundPool.setVolume(jumpSoundId, volume, volume) // Adjust volume for jump sound

soundPool.setVolume(coinSound
```

```
Id, volume, volume) // Adjust
volume for coin sound


soundPool.setVolume(gameOverS
oundId, volume, volume) //
Adjust volume for game over
sound

}
```

Releasing Resources

Ensure `SoundPool` resources are released when the activity is destroyed.

Kotlin

```
override fun onDestroy() {
    super.onDestroy()
```

```
        soundPool.release()      //
Release SoundPool resources

}
```

Step 5: Testing Your Game with Sound

Run your game and interact with it:

1. Jump your character and verify the jump sound plays.
2. Collect a coin and confirm the coin sound triggers.
3. Lose the game and listen for the game-over sound.

If sounds overlap or don't trigger correctly, adjust priorities or volumes in the `soundPool.play` method.

Step 6: Enhancing the Experience

To make the audio even more engaging:

Randomize Sound Effects: Use multiple variations of the same sound (e.g., different jump sounds) to avoid repetition. **Kotlin**

```
val jumpSounds = listOf(jumpSoundId1, jumpSoundId2, jumpSoundId3)

fun playRandomJumpSound() {
    val sound = jumpSounds.random()
    soundPool.play(sound, 1f, 1f, 0, 0, 1f)
}
```

1.

2. **Sync Audio with Animations:** Ensure sounds align perfectly with animations or actions in the game.

Chapter 9: Optimizing Game Performance

Creating a visually engaging and feature-rich game is exciting, but ensuring it runs smoothly is critical for player satisfaction. In this chapter, we'll focus on improving game performance by reducing lag, managing memory efficiently, and using debugging techniques to identify and fix bottlenecks. We'll also include actionable tips and code examples to guide you in optimizing your platformer game.

9.1 Reducing Lag and Improving FPS

Lag and low frame rates (FPS) can ruin the gaming experience. Here's how to optimize your game for a higher FPS and smoother gameplay.

1. Optimize the Game Loop

An efficient game loop is the backbone of smooth performance. If you're using a custom loop, ensure the frame timing calculations are accurate.

Example: Adjusting Frame Timing

Kotlin

```kotlin
var lastFrameTime = System.nanoTime()
val targetFPS = 60
val timePerFrame = 1_000_000_000 / targetFPS

fun gameLoop() {
    val currentTime = System.nanoTime()
```

```
    val    elapsedTime      =
currentTime - lastFrameTime

    if    (elapsedTime     >=
timePerFrame) {
       updateGame()        //
Update game logic
       renderGame()   // Draw
the frame
       lastFrameTime        =
currentTime
    } else {

Thread.sleep((timePerFrame   -
elapsedTime) / 1_000_000)   //
Sleep to maintain FPS
    }
}
```

2. Batch Draw Calls

Reduce the number of draw calls by grouping similar rendering tasks, such as drawing multiple objects with the same texture.

Example: Use a SpriteSheet Instead of loading individual images for animations or objects, use a spritesheet:

Kotlin

```
val spriteSheet = BitmapFactory.decodeResource(resources, R.drawable.spritesheet)

// Extract specific frames
val frame1 = Bitmap.createBitmap(spriteSheet, 0, 0, frameWidth, frameHeight)
val frame2 = Bitmap.createBitmap(spriteShe
```

```
et,      frameWidth,      0,
frameWidth, frameHeight)
```

---

3. Avoid Expensive Operations in Loops

Refrain from recalculating values inside loops. For instance, precompute values like collision boundaries or pre-load assets.

Tip: Cache objects and calculations:

Kotlin

```
val    playerBounds    =
Rect(player.x,    player.y,
player.x  +  player.width,
player.y + player.height)
```

---

4. Use Efficient Collision Detection

For collision-heavy games, avoid checking collisions between every object. Instead, use spatial partitioning techniques like a **grid-based system** or **quadtrees**.

Example: Simplified Grid-Based Detection

Kotlin

```
fun detectCollisions(objects: List<GameObject>, gridSize: Int): List<Pair<GameObject, GameObject>> {
    val grid = mutableMapOf<Pair<Int, Int>, MutableList<GameObject>>()

    // Assign objects to grid cells
    objects.forEach { obj ->
        val gridX = obj.x / gridSize
```

```
        val gridY = obj.y / gridSize
        grid.getOrPut(gridX to gridY) { mutableListOf() }.add(obj)
    }

    // Check for collisions only within the same grid cell
    val collisions = mutableListOf<Pair<GameObject, GameObject>>()
    grid.values.forEach { cellObjects ->
        for (i in cellObjects.indices) {
            for (j in i + 1 until cellObjects.size) {
                if (cellObjects[i].collidesWith(cellObjects[j])) {
```

```
collisions.add(cellObjects[i] 
to cellObjects[j])
                    }
                }
            }
        }

        return collisions
}
```

5. Reduce Resource Use

- **Compress Images:** Use optimized file formats (e.g., WebP for smaller image sizes).
- **Audio Optimization:** Compress audio files and load short effects with `SoundPool` instead of `MediaPlayer`.

9.2 Memory Management Tips

Poor memory management can lead to crashes and slowdowns. Here are best practices to avoid memory leaks and manage resources effectively.

1. Manage Bitmap Resources

Large bitmaps can hog memory. Always recycle unused bitmaps.

Kotlin

```
fun releaseBitmap(bitmap: Bitmap?) {
    if (bitmap != null && !bitmap.isRecycled) {
        bitmap.recycle()
    }
```

}

2. Use Object Pools

Object pools allow you to reuse objects instead of creating new ones repeatedly.

Example: Reusing Bullet Objects

Kotlin

```
class BulletPool {
    private val bullets = Stack<Bullet>()

    fun getBullet(): Bullet {
        return if (bullets.isEmpty()) Bullet()
        else bullets.pop()
    }
```

```kotlin
    fun releaseBullet(bullet: Bullet) {
        bullets.push(bullet)
    }
}
```

3. Avoid Memory Leaks

Watch out for long-lived references that can prevent garbage collection. Use weak references where appropriate.

Example: Avoid Leaks in Listeners

Kotlin

```kotlin
class MyActivity : Activity() {
```

```kotlin
    private val handler = Handler(Looper.getMainLooper())

    override fun onDestroy() {
        super.onDestroy()
        handler.removeCallbacksAndMessages(null) // Clear pending tasks
    }
}
```

---

4. Optimize Texture Loading

Load textures at appropriate resolutions for the device.

Kotlin

```
val             options                =
BitmapFactory.Options().apply
{
    inSampleSize   =   2    //
Reduce resolution by half
}
val        lowResBitmap         =
BitmapFactory.decodeResource(
resources,   R.drawable.image,
options)
```

9.3 Testing and Debugging Games

Debugging is a critical step to ensure your game runs smoothly across devices.

1. Use Debug Logs

Print logs to identify bottlenecks in performance.

Kotlin

```
Log.d("GameLoop", "Frame Time: $elapsedTime")
```

2. Profile Your Game

Use Android Studio's Profiler to monitor:

- CPU usage
- GPU rendering
- Memory allocation

3. Simulate Low-End Devices

Test your game on devices with less RAM or older GPUs by using Android Emulator's settings.

4. Catch Runtime Errors

Implement global error handling to log unexpected crashes.

Kotlin

```
Thread.setDefaultUncaughtExceptionHandler { thread, throwable ->
    Log.e("GameCrash", "Uncaught exception in thread ${thread.name}", throwable)
}
```

Project: Debug and Optimize Your Platformer Game for Smoother Gameplay

In this project, you'll take your platformer game to the next level by identifying and fixing performance issues, ensuring smooth gameplay, and making your game ready for players. Performance optimization is an art and a science, requiring careful analysis, efficient coding, and rigorous testing.

Let's work through the steps together, covering essential debugging and optimization techniques with practical examples.

Step 1: Profiling Your Game

The first step in debugging and optimization is identifying performance bottlenecks. Android Studio provides powerful tools for profiling your app's performance.

1. **Using the Android Studio Profiler**

   1. Open your project in Android Studio.
   2. Run your game on an emulator or physical device.
   3. Navigate to **View > Tool Windows > Profiler**.
   4. Select your app process to start profiling.

You'll see graphs for CPU, memory, network, and energy usage. Focus on:

- **CPU**: Identify functions consuming excessive processing power.
- **Memory**: Check for memory spikes that indicate potential leaks.
- **Frame Rendering**: Look for dropped frames caused by slow rendering.

2. **Analyzing the Output**

Here's what to watch for:

- High CPU usage during gameplay may indicate inefficient algorithms.
- Gradual memory increase suggests a memory leak.
- Low FPS (below 60) indicates rendering delays.

Tip: Use **Systrace** for detailed performance tracing, especially for rendering and input latency issues.

Step 2: Optimizing Performance

1. Improving Frame Rate

Lag or frame drops occur when your game loop takes too long to execute. Optimize your rendering logic and game updates.

Example: Efficient Game Loop

Kotlin

```kotlin
val targetFPS = 60

val timePerFrame = 1_000_000_000 / targetFPS

var lastFrameTime = System.nanoTime()


fun gameLoop() {

    val currentTime = System.nanoTime()

    val elapsedTime = currentTime - lastFrameTime


    if (elapsedTime >= timePerFrame) {
```

```
        updateGame()           // Update game state

        renderGame()   // Draw the frame

        lastFrameTime       = currentTime

    } else {

Thread.sleep((timePerFrame - elapsedTime) / 1_000_000)   // Maintain FPS

    }
}
```

2. Reducing Draw Calls

Batch rendering operations to minimize the number of draw calls. Use a spritesheet to combine multiple textures into a single image.

Example: Drawing from a Spritesheet

Kotlin

```
val spriteSheet = BitmapFactory.decodeResource(
resources,
R.drawable.spritesheet)

val sprite = Bitmap.createBitmap(spriteSheet, xOffset, yOffset, width, height)


canvas.drawBitmap(sprite, xPosition, yPosition, null)
```

3. Managing Resource Loading

Load assets asynchronously to avoid stalling the main thread.

Example: Loading Images in a Background Thread

Kotlin

```
val imageLoader = Executors.newSingleThreadExecutor()

var backgroundImage: Bitmap? = null


imageLoader.execute {
```

```
    backgroundImage           =
BitmapFactory.decodeResource(
resources,
R.drawable.background)
}
```

Step 3: Debugging Your Game

1. Logging for Debugging

Use `Logcat` to print debug messages during runtime.

Example: Logging Collisions

Kotlin

```
if (player.collidesWith(enemy)) {
    Log.d("Collision", "Player collided with enemy at ${player.x}, ${player.y}")
}
```

2. Handling Crashes Gracefully

Implement a global exception handler to log and recover from unexpected errors.

Example: Global Error Handler

Kotlin

```
Thread.setDefaultUncaughtExce
ptionHandler   {      thread,
throwable ->

    Log.e("CrashHandler",
"Error       in        thread
${thread.name}:
${throwable.message}")

}
```

Step 4: Optimizing Memory Usage

1. Avoid Memory Leaks

Release unused resources, such as bitmaps and audio files, when no longer needed.

Example: Recycling Bitmaps

Kotlin

```
fun recycleBitmap(bitmap: Bitmap?) {
    if (bitmap != null && !bitmap.isRecycled) {
        bitmap.recycle()
    }
}
```

2. Object Pooling

Reuse frequently created objects to reduce memory allocations.

Example: Bullet Pool

Kotlin

```kotlin
class BulletPool {

    private val pool = Stack<Bullet>()


    fun getBullet(): Bullet =
if (pool.isEmpty()) Bullet()
else pool.pop()


    fun releaseBullet(bullet: Bullet) {

        pool.push(bullet)

    }
}
```

Step 5: Testing Across Devices

1. Simulate Low-End Devices

Use the Android Emulator to simulate devices with lower RAM and slower CPUs. Adjust emulator settings:

- RAM: 1 GB
- CPU: Single core
- GPU: Disable hardware acceleration

2. Optimize for Screen Sizes

Test your game on devices with different screen sizes and aspect ratios. Use scalable assets and responsive layouts.

Final Task: Applying These Techniques

Now that you've learned the debugging and optimization process, apply these techniques to your platformer game.

1. **Profile Your Game:**
    - Identify areas consuming excessive CPU or memory.
2. **Optimize Rendering:**
    - Use batching and efficient drawing techniques.
3. **Test for Memory Leaks:**
    - Ensure all resources are released when no longer needed.
4. **Debug Runtime Errors:**
    - Fix any crashes or unexpected behavior.
5. **Validate Across Devices:**
    - Ensure smooth gameplay on both high-end and low-end hardware.

Debugging and optimization are iterative processes that involve profiling, analyzing, and improving your code. By following these steps, you'll ensure your platformer game delivers a seamless and enjoyable experience for players. The techniques you've learned here will serve you well in future projects, too.

Part 4:
Publishing and Monetizing
Your Game

Chapter 10: Preparing Your Game for Release

Congratulations! You've made it to the final stage of your game development journey—preparing your game for release. This chapter will guide you through testing your game across multiple devices, refining its graphics and sound, and finally packaging it for distribution. Let's ensure your platformer game shines for every player who gets to enjoy it.

10.1 Testing Your Game on Multiple Devices

Testing is critical to identify issues that may arise due to variations in hardware, software versions, screen sizes, and input methods. Comprehensive testing ensures a consistent experience for all users.

1. **Setting Up Your Testing Environment**

   - **Use Physical Devices:** Test your game on as many real Android devices as possible to simulate real-world usage.
   - **Utilize the Android Emulator:** Create multiple device profiles in Android Studio to emulate different screen sizes, resolutions, and performance levels.
   - **Cloud-Based Testing:** Platforms like Firebase Test Lab allow you to run tests on a wide range of devices without owning them.

2. **Key Areas to Test**

   - **Performance:** Check for lag, stuttering, and responsiveness.
   - **Graphics Scaling:** Ensure UI and game elements are displayed correctly on various screen sizes.

- **Audio Quality:** Verify that sound effects and background music work as intended without distortion or delays.
- **User Input:** Test touch inputs, gestures, and multi-touch capabilities.

3. Automating Tests

Automated tests save time and help catch regressions.

Example: Writing a UI Test

Kotlin

```kotlin
@RunWith(AndroidJUnit4::class)
class GameUITest {
    @Test
    fun testGameLaunches() {
```

```
        val      scenario      =
ActivityScenario.launch(MainA
ctivity::class.java)


onView(withId(R.id.startButto
n)).check(matches(isDisplayed
()))
    }
}
```

Run tests using the command:

bash

```
./gradlew
connectedAndroidTest
```

4. Real-World Usage

Encourage friends or beta testers to play your game and provide feedback. Track issues like unexpected crashes or confusing controls.

10.2 Finalizing Graphics and Sound Quality

Polished visuals and audio are key to delivering a professional experience. Let's refine these elements to perfection.

1. Graphics Optimization

- **Texture Compression:** Use tools like Android's ASTC format to compress textures without sacrificing quality.

- **High-Resolution Assets:** Provide assets for different screen densities (e.g., `mdpi`, `hdpi`, `xhdpi`, `xxhdpi`).
- **Eliminate Artifacts:** Ensure all sprites are clean, without jagged edges or unintended transparency.

Example: Adding Density-Specific Drawables Place your images in the following directories:

bash

```
res/drawable-mdpi/

res/drawable-hdpi/

res/drawable-xhdpi/

res/drawable-xxhdpi/
```

2. Audio Refinement

- **Normalize Volume Levels:** Ensure consistent audio levels across all effects and music.
- **Compress Audio Files:** Use formats like OGG or MP3 to reduce file sizes while maintaining quality.
- **Avoid Looping Issues:** Verify that background music loops smoothly.

Example: Adding Background Music

Kotlin

```
val mediaPlayer = MediaPlayer.create(context, R.raw.background_music)
```

```
mediaPlayer.isLooping = true
mediaPlayer.start()
```

Project: Final Testing and Packaging Your Platformer Game

Now it's time to tie everything together. This project will guide you through the final steps to ensure your game is polished, bug-free, and ready for release.

Step 1: Conduct Rigorous Testing

1. **Device Compatibility:** Test on at least three devices with varying specifications (e.g., low-end, mid-range, high-end).
2. **Stress Test:** Simulate heavy loads by running the game for extended periods and observing memory or performance issues.

3. **Edge Cases:** Test scenarios like pausing the game during a phone call or switching between apps.

Step 2: Optimize Game Assets

- Revisit all images and audio files to ensure they are compressed and properly scaled.
- Remove unused assets to reduce the APK size.

Step 3: Configure App Permissions

Ensure your app requests only the necessary permissions. For example:

xml

```xml
<uses-permission
android:name="android.permiss
ion.INTERNET"/>

<uses-permission
android:name="android.permiss
ion.WAKE_LOCK"/>
```

Step 4: Build and Sign the APK

To release your game, you need to generate a signed APK or App Bundle.

Generating a Signed APK:

1. Go to **Build > Generate Signed Bundle / APK**.
2. Choose **APK** or **App Bundle**.
3. Follow the prompts to select your key store and credentials.
4. Complete the process to generate your signed APK.

Command-Line Option:

bash

```
./gradlew assembleRelease
```

Step 5: Upload to Google Play Console

1. Create a developer account at the Google Play Console.
2. Follow the steps to create a new app:
   - Upload your APK/App Bundle.
   - Fill out the store listing details (title, description, screenshots).
   - Set pricing and distribution preferences.
3. Submit your app for review.

Final testing and packaging are vital steps in delivering a smooth and enjoyable gaming experience to players. With your platformer game debugged, optimized, and polished, you're now ready to share it with the world. The skills you've gained will help you confidently tackle future game development projects.

Chapter 11: Publishing to Google Play Store

Publishing your game on the Google Play Store is an exciting milestone. It allows you to share your work with a global audience and potentially monetize your efforts. In this chapter, we'll cover everything from creating a developer account to writing an effective app description. We'll also walk you through submitting your platformer game to the Play Store.

11.1 Creating a Developer Account

To publish your app, you need a Google Play Developer Account.

1. Steps to Create Your Account

1. **Sign Up:**
    - Go to the Google Play Console.

- Sign in with your Google account.

2. **Pay the Registration Fee:**
    - A one-time payment of $25 is required. This fee grants lifetime access to the developer console.

3. **Provide Developer Details:**
    - Fill in your account information, including your name, email, and contact details. Ensure accuracy, as this information will appear on the Play Store.

2. Accept Developer Agreement

Carefully review and accept Google's Developer Distribution Agreement.

3. Set Up a Merchant Account (Optional)

If you plan to monetize your game, set up a merchant account via the Google Play Console. This enables you to process payments for in-app purchases or paid downloads.

11.2 App Bundles and APK Files

The Google Play Store requires you to upload your game in either an **App Bundle** or **APK** format. Let's discuss these formats and how to prepare them.

1. App Bundle vs. APK

- **App Bundle:** A packaging format that contains all resources and code for your app. The Play Store uses it to generate device-specific APKs, optimizing app size.
- **APK:** A standalone Android Package file. While still accepted, App Bundles are now the preferred format.

2. Preparing an App Bundle

1. Open your project in Android Studio.

2. Go to **Build > Build Bundle(s)/APK(s) > Build Bundle(s)**.
3. Once the process is complete, locate your App Bundle in the `output` directory.

Command-Line Option:

bash

```
./gradlew bundleRelease
```

3. Generating a Signed APK

If you prefer an APK:

1. Go to **Build > Generate Signed Bundle / APK**.
2. Choose **APK**.

3. Follow the prompts to use your key store credentials (or create one if necessary).

11.3 Writing an Effective App Description

An engaging app description can attract more downloads. It should highlight the key features and appeal to your target audience.

1. Structure Your Description

- **Opening Line:** Summarize your game in one sentence. Example: *"Dive into a thrilling platformer adventure packed with levels, challenges, and fun animations!"*
- **Features:** Use bullet points to highlight gameplay mechanics, graphics, and sound quality.

- **Call-to-Action:** Encourage users to download. Example: *"Download now and start your adventure!"*

2. Keywords and Localization

- Include relevant keywords to improve search visibility.
- Translate your description into other languages to reach a broader audience.

Project: Submit Your Platformer Game to the Play Store

It's time to upload your game to the Play Store! Follow these steps to ensure a smooth submission process.

Step 1: Prepare Your Assets

Before uploading, gather the following:

- **App Icon:** A 512x512px PNG file.

- **Screenshots:** At least 2-8 images showcasing gameplay. Recommended resolutions: 1080x1920px or higher.
- **Feature Graphic (Optional):** A banner image (1024x500px) that represents your game.

Step 2: Upload Your Game

1. **Create a New App:**
    - Log in to the Google Play Console.
    - Select **Create App**, then fill in basic information like your app's title and default language.
2. **Upload the App Bundle/APK:**
    - Navigate to the **Release > Production** section.
    - Upload your App Bundle or APK file.

Step 3: Complete the Store Listing

1. Fill in the app's **title**, **short description**, and **full description**.
2. Upload the required visuals (icon, screenshots, and feature graphic).
3. Select a **content rating** by completing the Google questionnaire.

Step 4: Set Pricing and Distribution

- Choose whether your game is **free** or **paid**.
- Select the countries where your game will be available.
- Specify if your game contains ads or in-app purchases.

Step 5: Submit for Review

- Double-check all details.
- Click **Submit for Review**. The review process usually takes a few days.

Publishing your game on the Google Play Store is a rewarding step that transforms your hard work into a sharable experience. By following the guidelines in this chapter, you'll ensure your game is polished, optimized, and ready to reach players worldwide. With your platformer game live on the Play Store, you're officially a published game developer.

Chapter 12: Monetizing Your Game

Creating a game is rewarding, but monetizing it effectively ensures your hard work pays off financially. This chapter covers the most popular strategies for monetization, including ads, in-app purchases, and alternative revenue streams. By the end, you'll be equipped to generate income from your games without compromising user experience.

12.1 Implementing Ads

Ads are one of the most accessible ways to monetize your game. You can integrate different ad types depending on your game's design and user engagement goals.

1. Ad Types Overview

- **Banner Ads:** Small, static ads displayed at the top or bottom of the screen. Ideal for casual games.
- **Interstitial Ads:** Full-screen ads that appear at natural pauses (e.g., between levels).
- **Rewarded Ads:** Ads that offer in-game rewards (e.g., extra lives) in exchange for viewing.

2. Integrating Google AdMob

Google AdMob is a popular platform for in-game ads.

a. Add the AdMob SDK

In your project's `build.gradle` file (app-level), add the following dependency:
gradle

```
implementation
```

```
'com.google.android.gms:play-
services-ads:22.3.0'
```

1.
2. Sync your project with Gradle.

b. Initialize the Mobile Ads SDK

Add the initialization code in your `MainActivity`:

Kotlin

```
import
com.google.android.gms.ads.Mo
bileAds

override                    fun
onCreate(savedInstanceState:
Bundle?) {

super.onCreate(savedInstanceS
tate)
```

```
setContentView(R.layout.activity_main)

    // Initialize AdMob
MobileAds.initialize(this) {}
}
```

c. Load and Display Ads

Banner Ad Example

Add an AdView to your XML layout:
xml

```
<com.google.android.gms.ads.AdView
    android:id="@+id/adView"

android:layout_width="match_parent"
```

```
    android:layout_height="wrap_content"
    ads:adSize="BANNER"
    ads:adUnitId="YOUR_BANNER_AD_UNIT_ID" />
```

In your MainActivity:

Kotlin

```
import com.google.android.gms.ads.AdRequest

val adView = findViewById<AdView>(R.id.adView)
val adRequest = AdRequest.Builder().build()
adView.loadAd(adRequest)
```

-

Rewarded Ad Example Kotlin

```kotlin
import com.google.android.gms.ads.rewarded.RewardedAd
import com.google.android.gms.ads.rewarded.RewardItem
import com.google.android.gms.ads.AdRequest

lateinit var rewardedAd: RewardedAd

private fun loadRewardedAd() {
    rewardedAd = RewardedAd(this, "YOUR_REWARDED_AD_UNIT_ID")
```

```kotlin
    val adRequest = AdRequest.Builder().build()

rewardedAd.loadAd(adRequest, object : RewardedAdLoadCallback() {
        override fun onRewardedAdLoaded() {
            // Ad successfully loaded
        }

        override fun onRewardedAdFailedToLoad(errorCode: Int) {
            // Handle the error
        }
    })
}
```

```kotlin
private fun showRewardedAd() {
    if (rewardedAd.isLoaded) {
        rewardedAd.show(this) { rewardItem: RewardItem ->
            // Grant the reward
        }
    }
}
```

-

12.2 Setting Up In-App Purchases

In-app purchases (IAPs) allow players to buy virtual goods, such as power-ups or premium features. This approach often generates more revenue than ads.

1. Add the Google Play Billing Library

In your `build.gradle` file (app-level), add:

gradle

```
implementation
'com.android.billingclient:bi
lling:6.0.1'
```

2. Create Products in the Play Console

1. Go to the **Google Play Console**.
2. Under **Monetize** > **Products**, create in-app items (e.g., consumables like coins or non-consumables like premium levels).

3. Implement Billing in Your App

a. Set Up BillingClient
Kotlin

```kotlin
import com.android.billingclient.api.*

lateinit var billingClient: BillingClient

private fun setupBillingClient() {
    billingClient = BillingClient.newBuilder(this)
        .setListener { billingResult, purchases ->
            // Handle purchase updates
        }
        .enablePendingPurchases()
        .build()
}
```

b. Query Products

Retrieve available in-app products:

Kotlin

```kotlin
val skuList = listOf("your_product_id_1", "your_product_id_2")
val params = SkuDetailsParams.newBuilder()
    .setSkusList(skuList)
    .setType(BillingClient.SkuType.INAPP)
billingClient.querySkuDetailsAsync(params.build()) { billingResult, skuDetailsList ->
    skuDetailsList?.forEach { skuDetails ->
        // Display product details in the game
```

        }
}

c. Handle Purchases

Initiate a purchase:

Kotlin

```
val        flowParams     = BillingFlowParams.newBuilder()

.setSkuDetails(selectedSkuDetails)
    .build()
billingClient.launchBillingFlow(this, flowParams)
```

12.3 Exploring Alternative Revenue Streams

Beyond ads and IAPs, consider these options:

1. Premium Version of the Game

Offer a paid version with additional features or ad-free gameplay.

2. Merchandise

If your game becomes popular, sell related merchandise like t-shirts, mugs, or posters.

3. Subscription Model

Charge users monthly for premium features, exclusive levels, or early access to updates.

4. Sponsorships and Partnerships

Collaborate with brands for in-game promotions or sponsorships.

5. Crowdfunding

Use platforms like Patreon or Kickstarter to gather support from your fanbase.

Part 5:
Expanding Your Skills

Chapter 13: Exploring 3D Game Development Basics

Moving into the realm of 3D game development opens up a world of possibilities for creating immersive and visually captivating experiences. In this chapter, we'll cover the essentials of 3D graphics in Android, explore the tools and frameworks available for building 3D games, and provide practical guidance to help you get started.

Introduction to 3D Graphics in Android

Stepping into 3D graphics on Android opens up exciting opportunities to create immersive and engaging experiences. Unlike 2D graphics, which operate on flat surfaces, 3D graphics simulate depth, allowing you to render objects in a virtual space that can mimic the real world or imaginative environments.

This chapter introduces the fundamentals of 3D graphics in Android, provides essential concepts, and demonstrates a simple 3D implementation using **OpenGL ES**, the backbone of Android's 3D rendering capabilities.

Understanding 3D Graphics

3D graphics involve representing objects in a three-dimensional space using a combination of mathematical models and rendering techniques. Here are key aspects to understand:

1. The 3D Coordinate System

- 3D space uses three axes:
    - **X-axis**: Horizontal (left/right)

- o **Y-axis**: Vertical (up/down)
- o **Z-axis**: Depth (in/out of the screen)
- Every object or point in 3D space is defined by its `(x, y, z)` coordinates.

2. Vertices and Polygons

- Vertices: The corner points of a shape in 3D space.
- **Polygons**: Surfaces formed by connecting vertices. Most 3D graphics use triangles as the basic building blocks for objects.

3. Rendering Pipeline

The rendering pipeline is the process of converting 3D models into 2D images on your screen. Key stages include:

- **Model Transformation**: Positioning objects in 3D space.

- **View Transformation**: Placing a virtual camera to determine the viewpoint.
- **Projection**: Mapping 3D coordinates to a 2D plane for rendering.
- **Rasterization**: Converting vector data into pixels.

3D Rendering in Android: OpenGL ES

Android supports 3D graphics through **OpenGL ES (Embedded Systems)**, a lightweight version of OpenGL designed for mobile devices. OpenGL ES 2.0+ is commonly used for modern game development.

Getting Started with OpenGL ES

To use OpenGL ES in an Android project:

Add OpenGL ES to Your Project Ensure your `AndroidManifest.xml` specifies

OpenGL ES support: xml

```
<uses-feature 
android:glEsVersion="0x00020000" android:required="true" />
```

1.
2. **Create a Custom GLSurfaceView** A `GLSurfaceView` is a surface that renders OpenGL graphics.

Example: Setting Up a Basic 3D Scene

This example demonstrates how to render a spinning colored triangle in OpenGL ES.

Step 1: Create a GLSurfaceView

The `GLSurfaceView` provides a surface where OpenGL ES renders the 3D content.

```java
import android.content.Context;
import android.opengl.GLSurfaceView;

public class MyGLSurfaceView extends GLSurfaceView {
    public MyGLSurfaceView(Context context) {
        super(context);
```

```
        // Set OpenGL ES 2.0 context

setEGLContextClientVersion(2);


        // Set the renderer for drawing

        setRenderer(new MyGLRenderer());

    }

}
```

Step 2: Implement a Renderer

The GLRenderer defines how to draw the scene and handle frame updates.

java

```java
import android.opengl.GLES20;

import javax.microedition.khronos.egl.EGLConfig;

import javax.microedition.khronos.opengles.GL10;


public class MyGLRenderer implements GLSurfaceView.Renderer {

    private Triangle triangle;
```

```
    @Override
    public void onSurfaceCreated(GL10 gl, EGLConfig config) {
        // Set clear color (background)
        GLES20.glClearColor(0.0f, 0.0f, 0.0f, 1.0f);

        // Initialize the triangle
        triangle = new Triangle();
    }
```

```java
    @Override
    public                void onDrawFrame(GL10 gl) {
        // Clear the screen
GLES20.glClear(GLES20.GL_COLOR_BUFFER_BIT);

        // Draw the triangle
        triangle.draw();
    }

    @Override
    public                void onSurfaceChanged(GL10 gl, int width, int height) {
```

```
        //      Adjust      the viewport
        GLES20.glViewport(0, 0, width, height);
    }
}
```

Step 3: Define the Triangle

The triangle is a basic 3D object created using vertices.

java

```
import java.nio.ByteBuffer;
import java.nio.ByteOrder;
import java.nio.FloatBuffer;
```

```java
import android.opengl.GLES20;

public class Triangle {
    private FloatBuffer vertexBuffer;
    private final int program;


    // Triangle vertices (X, Y, Z)
    private static final float[] vertices = {
        0.0f, 0.6f, 0.0f, // Top
        -0.5f, -0.3f, 0.0f, // Bottom left
```

```
            0.5f,    -0.3f,   0.0f  // Bottom right
    };


    // Vertex shader code
    private static final String vertexShaderCode =
            "attribute vec4 vPosition;" +
            "void main() {" +
            "  gl_Position = vPosition;" +
            "}";


    // Fragment shader code
```

```java
    private static final String fragmentShaderCode =
        "precision mediump float;" +
        "uniform vec4 vColor;" +
        "void main() {" +
        "  gl_FragColor = vColor;" +
        "}";

    // Triangle color (red)
    private final float[] color = {1.0f, 0.0f, 0.0f, 1.0f};
```

```
public Triangle() {
    // Allocate buffer for vertices
    ByteBuffer bb = ByteBuffer.allocateDirect(vertices.length * 4);
    bb.order(ByteOrder.nativeOrder());
    vertexBuffer = bb.asFloatBuffer();
    vertexBuffer.put(vertices);
    vertexBuffer.position(0);
```

```
// Compile shaders and link program
int vertexShader = loadShader(GLES20.GL_VERTEX_SHADER, vertexShaderCode);
int fragmentShader = loadShader(GLES20.GL_FRAGMENT_SHADER, fragmentShaderCode);
program = GLES20.glCreateProgram();

GLES20.glAttachShader(program, vertexShader);

GLES20.glAttachShader(program, fragmentShader);
```

```
GLES20.glLinkProgram(program);
    }

    public void draw() {
        // Use the program
GLES20.glUseProgram(program);

        // Pass vertex data
        int positionHandle = GLES20.glGetAttribLocation(program, "vPosition");

GLES20.glEnableVertexAttribArray(positionHandle);
```

```
GLES20.glVertexAttribPointer(
positionHandle,           3,
GLES20.GL_FLOAT,  false,  0,
vertexBuffer);


        // Pass color data
        int   colorHandle   =
GLES20.glGetUniformLocation(p
rogram, "vColor");


GLES20.glUniform4fv(colorHand
le, 1, color, 0);


        // Draw the triangle

GLES20.glDrawArrays(GLES20.GL
_TRIANGLES, 0, 3);
```

```
        // Disable vertex array

GLES20.glDisableVertexAttribArray(positionHandle);
    }


    private int loadShader(int type, String shaderCode) {

        int shader = GLES20.glCreateShader(type);

GLES20.glShaderSource(shader, shaderCode);
```

```
GLES20.glCompileShader(shader
);

        return shader;

    }

}
```

Tools and Frameworks for 3D Games

Building 3D games for Android can feel daunting, but with the right tools and frameworks, the process becomes more accessible, efficient, and fun. From rendering engines to game development environments, there are powerful resources to help you bring your 3D game ideas to life.

In this chapter, we'll explore the most widely used tools and frameworks for 3D game development on Android, focusing on their strengths and how to use them effectively.

---

1. LibGDX

LibGDX is a robust Java-based framework for developing 2D and 3D games. It's highly versatile and offers cross-platform support, making it a favorite among developers looking for control over every aspect of their game.

Key Features

- Cross-platform deployment (Android, iOS, Desktop, and Web).
- 3D rendering support for meshes, textures, and shaders.
- Built-in physics engines (Box2D and Bullet Physics).
- Scene management and advanced input handling.

How to Get Started with LibGDX for 3D Development

Set Up a New Project Use the LibGDX project generator to set up a base project:
bash

```
java -jar gdx-setup.jar
```

Basic 3D Scene in LibGDX Here's an example of rendering a spinning cube:
java

```
import com.badlogic.gdx.ApplicationAdapter;

import com.badlogic.gdx.Gdx;

import com.badlogic.gdx.graphics.GL20;
```

```
import com.badlogic.gdx.graphics.PerspectiveCamera;
import com.badlogic.gdx.graphics.g3d.Environment;
import com.badlogic.gdx.graphics.g3d.Model;
import com.badlogic.gdx.graphics.g3d.ModelBatch;
import com.badlogic.gdx.graphics.g3d.ModelInstance;
import com.badlogic.gdx.graphics.g3d.attributes.ColorAttribute;
```

```java
import com.badlogic.gdx.graphics.g3d.environment.DirectionalLight;

import com.badlogic.gdx.graphics.g3d.utils.ModelBuilder;


public class My3DGame extends ApplicationAdapter {

    private PerspectiveCamera camera;

    private ModelBatch modelBatch;

    private Model model;

    private ModelInstance cube;
```

```java
    private         Environment
environment;


    @Override

    public void create() {

        // Initialize camera

        camera        =        new
PerspectiveCamera(67,
Gdx.graphics.getWidth(),
Gdx.graphics.getHeight());

camera.position.set(3f,    3f,
3f);

        camera.lookAt(0f,  0f,
0f);

        camera.near = 1f;

        camera.far = 300f;
```

```
camera.update();


// Initialize environment and lighting
    environment = new Environment();
    environment.set(new ColorAttribute(ColorAttribute.AmbientLight, 0.8f, 0.8f, 0.8f, 1f));
    environment.add(new DirectionalLight().set(1f, 1f, 1f, -1f, -0.8f, -0.2f));


// Create a cube model
```

```
ModelBuilder modelBuilder = new ModelBuilder();

model = modelBuilder.createBox(1f, 1f, 1f,

               new Material(ColorAttribute.createDiffuse(ColorAttribute.Diffuse, 0, 1, 0, 1)),

Usage.Position | Usage.Normal);

cube = new ModelInstance(model);


modelBatch = new ModelBatch();
```

        }

        @Override

        public void render() {

            // Clear the screen

Gdx.gl.glClear(GL20.GL_COLOR_BUFFER_BIT | GL20.GL_DEPTH_BUFFER_BIT);

            // Rotate the cube

cube.transform.rotate(0f, 1f, 0f, 1f);

            // Render the cube

```
modelBatch.begin(camera);

modelBatch.render(cube, environment);

        modelBatch.end();

    }


    @Override

    public void dispose() {

        modelBatch.dispose();

        model.dispose();

    }

}
```

This code sets up a spinning green cube, giving you a taste of 3D rendering in LibGDX.

---

2. Unity

Unity is one of the most popular game engines in the world, known for its user-friendly interface and extensive features. It supports both 2D and 3D development and is especially powerful for Android 3D game development.

Key Features

- Drag-and-drop editor with a visual scripting option.
- Asset Store with thousands of prebuilt models, textures, and tools.
- Cross-platform deployment with a single codebase.
- Extensive support for physics, animation, and AI.

Getting Started with Unity for Android

1. **Install Unity Hub** Download Unity Hub from the official website and install the Android Build Support module.
2. **Create a New 3D Project** Open Unity Hub, click "New Project," and select "3D."
3. **Add a Cube to the Scene** In Unity's editor:
    - Right-click the hierarchy and choose `3D Object → Cube`.
    - Adjust its position, scale, and rotation using the inspector.

Script a Simple Rotation Add a C# script to rotate the cube: csharp

```
using UnityEngine;
```

```
public class RotateCube : MonoBehaviour {

    public float speed = 50f;

    void Update() {

transform.Rotate(Vector3.up, speed * Time.deltaTime);

    }
}
```

4. Attach this script to the cube, and it will spin automatically.

Unity's visual editor simplifies complex tasks, such as handling animations or adding lighting effects, making it a powerful option for beginners and professionals alike.

3. Unreal Engine

Unreal Engine (UE) is another industry-standard game engine known for high-fidelity graphics and performance. Although heavier than Unity, it offers unparalleled visual quality.

Key Features

- Blueprints: A visual scripting system that requires no coding.
- Photorealistic rendering with advanced lighting and material systems.
- Free-to-use with royalty-based licensing.

Quick Start with Unreal Engine for Android

1. **Install Unreal Engine** Download the Epic Games Launcher and install Unreal Engine with Android SDK support.
2. **Create a New Project** Select the "Third Person" template to start with a prebuilt character and environment.

3. **Modify Blueprints** Open the character blueprint, and add custom movement or interaction logic without writing a single line of code.

While Unreal Engine has a steep learning curve, it's an excellent choice for developers focusing on highly polished and performance-intensive games.

---

4. Blender for 3D Asset Creation

Blender is an open-source 3D modeling and animation tool widely used for creating game assets. You can model, texture, and animate 3D objects, then export them into game engines like Unity or LibGDX.

Key Features

- Powerful 3D modeling tools.
- Animation and rigging capabilities.

- Support for exporting assets in formats like `.fbx` and `.obj`.

Basic Workflow

1. Create your 3D model in Blender.
2. Apply textures and materials.
3. Export the model to `.fbx` or `.obj`.
4. Import it into your game engine for use.

Choosing the Right Tool for Your Project

- Use **LibGDX** if you prefer coding everything and want lightweight cross-platform support.
- Choose **Unity** if you value a beginner-friendly environment with an extensive asset store and visual editor.
- Opt for **Unreal Engine** for projects that demand cutting-edge graphics and performance.

- Use **Blender** alongside any engine for custom asset creation.

The tools and frameworks you choose will shape your game development journey. Each offers unique strengths, so pick the one that best aligns with your project's goals and your level of experience. Once you've chosen your toolset, you'll be ready to build stunning 3D worlds and bring them to life on Android.

Appendices

Appendix A: Troubleshooting Common Errors

Developing games often involves tackling errors and debugging challenges. Here's a quick guide to resolve some common issues:

1. Gradle Build Errors

- **Error Message:** *"Gradle Sync Failed"*
    - **Solution:**
        - Ensure your Android Studio and Gradle versions are compatible.
        - Delete the `gradle` folder in your project and re-sync.
        - Check for missing dependencies in the `build.gradle` file.

- **Error Message:** *"Cannot resolve symbol"*
  - **Solution:**
    - Rebuild the project using `Build > Rebuild Project`.
    - Invalidate caches in Android Studio: `File > Invalidate Caches / Restart`.

2. Memory Leaks

- **Issue:** App crashes due to high memory usage.
  - **Solution:**
    - Use `Android Profiler` to analyze memory usage.
    - Avoid holding references to context in static variables.

- Use `WeakReference` when necessary.

3. Render Lag or Low FPS

- **Issue:** The game feels sluggish.
    - **Solution:**
        - Optimize the number of draw calls.
        - Reduce the complexity of 3D models and textures.
        - Use object pooling for frequently instantiated objects.

4. Audio Not Playing

- **Issue:** Sound effects or background music fail to play.
    - **Solution:**
        - Ensure audio files are in supported formats (`.ogg` or `.mp3`).

- Check that the file paths in your code are correct.
- Use `MediaPlayer` or `SoundPool` for proper audio handling.

5. Touch or Gesture Issues

- **Issue:** Unresponsive gestures or incorrect touch inputs.
    - **Solution:**
        - Verify touch coordinates using logs.
        - Test gesture handling in different screen resolutions.

Appendix B: Sample Game Code and Links

Here are links to sample projects and snippets to inspire your development journey.

Sample Game Code

1. **Basic 2D Game Template (Catch the Ball)**
    - Repository: [GitHub: Catch the Ball](#)
    - Features: Basic player movement, collision detection, and scoring.
2. **Platformer Game (Multi-Level Example)**
    - Repository: [GitHub: Platformer Game](#)
    - Features: Multi-level support, power-ups, enemies, and scoring.
3. **3D Game Starter (LibGDX)**
    - Repository: [GitHub: 3D Starter](#)

- Features: Simple 3D scene setup and animations.

Additional Resources

- **Android Documentation:** developer.android.com
- **Unity Tutorials**: unity.com/learn
- **Unreal Engine Resources**: unrealengine.com

Appendix C: Glossary of Key Terms

1. Frame Per Second (FPS): The number of frames rendered per second. Higher FPS results in smoother visuals.

2. Game Loop: A continuous cycle that updates the game state and renders graphics to the screen.

3. Gradle: A build tool used in Android development to automate tasks such as compiling code and managing dependencies.

4. Object Pooling: A technique to reuse objects to minimize memory allocation and garbage collection during gameplay.

5. Shader: A program that defines how to render surfaces in a game, controlling lighting, shadows, and textures.

6. Texture: An image applied to the surface of a 2D or 3D object to give it visual detail.

7. Gesture Recognition: The process of interpreting user inputs such as swipes, pinches, and multi-touch actions.

8. Physics Engine: A system that simulates real-world physics in a game, such as gravity, collisions, and velocity.

9. Render Pipeline: The sequence of steps that transform 3D models into a 2D image on the screen.

10. Asset: Any resource used in a game, such as graphics, sounds, or scripts.

11. App Bundle: A publishing format for Android that includes all your app's compiled code and resources.

12. APK (Android Package): A file format used to distribute and install apps on Android devices.

13. MediaPlayer: A class in Android for playing media files such as audio and video.

14. SoundPool: A class in Android designed to handle multiple audio streams efficiently.

15. Debugging: The process of identifying and fixing errors in your code.

With these appendices, you'll have the tools and knowledge to troubleshoot issues, access valuable resources, and understand key game development terms. These will be indispensable as you continue your journey to mastering Android game development.

www.ingramcontent.com/pod-product-compliance
Lightning Source LLC
Chambersburg PA
CBHW071651240526

45469CB0002IB/1937